YORK NOTES

NINETEEN EIGHTY-FOUR

GEORGE ORWELL

NOTES BY MICHAEL SHERBORNE

I0653005

 Longman

York Press

The right of Michael Sherborne to be identified as Author
of this Work has been asserted by him in accordance with the
Copyright, Designs and Patents Act 1988

YORK PRESS
322 Old Brompton Road, London SW5 9JH

PEARSON EDUCATION LIMITED
Edinburgh Gate, Harlow,
Essex CM20 2JE, United Kingdom
Associated companies, branches and representatives throughout the world

First published 2001
This new and fully revised edition first published 2005
Third impression 2006

10 9 8 7 6 5 4 3

ISBN-10: 1-4058-0704-0
ISBN-13: 978-1-4058-0704-3

Typeset by Land & Unwin (Data Sciences), Bugbrooke, Northamptonshire
Produced by Pearson Education Asia Limited, Hong Kong

CONTENTS

PART FOUR
CRITICAL HISTORY

PART FIVE
BACKGROUND

PART ONE

INTRODUCTION

HOW TO STUDY A NOVEL

Studying a novel on your own requires self-discipline and a carefully thought-out work plan in order to be effective.

- You will need to read the novel more than once. Start by reading it quickly for pleasure, then read it slowly and thoroughly.

- On your second reading make detailed notes on the plot, characters and themes of the novel. Further readings will generate new ideas and help you to memorise the details of the story.

- Some of the characters will develop as the plot unfolds. How do your responses towards them change during the course of the novel?

- Think about how the novel is narrated. From whose point of view are events described?

- A novel may or may not present events chronologically: the time-scheme may be a key to its structure and organisation.

- What part do the settings play in the novel?

- Are words, images or incidents repeated so as to give the work a pattern? Do such patterns help you to understand the novel's themes?

- Identify what styles of language are used in the novel.

- What is the effect of the novel's ending? Is the action completed and closed, or left incomplete and open?

- Does the novel present a moral and just world?

- Cite exact sources for all quotations, whether from the text itself or from critical commentaries. Wherever possible find your own examples from the novel to back up your opinions.

- Always express your ideas in your own words.

These York Notes offer an introduction to *Nineteen Eighty-Four* and cannot substitute for close reading of the text and the study of secondary sources.

CHECK THE BOOK

Michael McKeon's *Theory of the Novel: A Historical Approach* (2000) is an excellent introduction to the history of the novel.

READING *NINETEEN EIGHTY-FOUR*

In the second half of the twentieth century *Nineteen Eighty-Four* was one of the best-known and most frequently cited books in the world. Whether its reputation will remain as high in the twenty-first century is an open question. As its title indicates, it is to some extent a topical book and the way readers approach it is therefore bound to change with time.

Before the year 1984, the book *Nineteen Eighty-Four* was commonly seen as prophecy, a warning about the drift of civilisation towards ever stronger state control. Journalists and politicians quoted from it, **science fiction** writers imitated it, almost as though Orwell's word had the authority of revealed truth. Since the year 1984, and even more since the fall of East European Communism in 1989, the book has ceased to look like a prediction, leaving it more open to assessment as a work of literature. Yet we still cannot read it without being aware that it has a forceful message and that, to some extent, our response to the message will continue to govern our assessment of its literary value. The best course for readers in this uncertain situation has to be to pay careful attention to the text, to think for themselves and to remember that a genuinely good book is one which is bound to have many facets.

One important aspect of *Nineteen Eighty-Four* is that it is a historical document. It reflects the despair of the 1930s and 1940s as hopes for political and economic progress were dashed, capitalism became mired in a seemingly endless depression and totalitarianism threatened to engulf Europe. Even as the Fascists were beaten down, Communism rose up as a renewed threat to liberal democracy and Orwell's vivid depiction of the modern single-party dictatorship was felt by many to be a timely warning. We can legitimately read the book, therefore, as a reflection of the era in which it was written (1984 mirroring 1948). However, that does not necessarily mean that we have to consign it to the archives as obsolete, along with the newspaper editorials and political manifestos of its time. The targets of Orwell's criticism and **satire** are far too serious to date easily.

 CHECK THE BOOK

George Woodcock in Part 4 of *The Crystal Spirit: A Study of George Orwell* (1967) notes how deeply *Nineteen Eighty-Four* is rooted in 1948. It is 'a novel about the future, but the future conceived as a degenerated present'.

Winston points out that the year in which he is living may not actually be 1984 at all. (It is therefore referred to sceptically in these Notes as '1984', escorted at all times by a vigilant pair of inverted commas.) Similarly, O'Brien claims that the philosophy of the ruling Party is better than that of Fascism or Communism, making it clear that the book is not simply about those two movements but about the philosophical and political attitudes which lie behind them. There are still plenty of pretentious dictatorships in the world today for which the Party can stand as a kind of ultimate version. No one has succeeded better than Orwell in evoking the world of the self-styled charismatic leader and his secret police, presiding over a malfunctioning economy, pumping out vacuous propaganda and crushing anyone with the temerity to question their regime. Cruel political oppression is shown in all its horror and all its absurdity. However, if totalitarian rule is the book's main target, it is not its only one.

After all, O'Brien is less like an interrogator than he is like 'a doctor, a teacher, even a priest' (Part Three, Chapter 2, p. 257). These comparisons should not be taken lightly. Today there are still religious movements, great and small, for whom God and worldly power seem interchangeable and which employ brainwashing tactics as ruthlessly as O'Brien does. There are still therapists who thrive on the dependency of their patients and try to change their perceptions and behaviour using drugs and electric shocks. At the risk of stretching the point, there are even university lecturers in English who assert that authors (like Winston with his diary) cannot generate meanings of their own, claiming instead that language 'writes' the author, as Newspeak aspires to do, and that there is no one reality which we all share but only warring 'interpretative communities', intellectual superstates competing for our allegiance.

Nineteen Eighty-Four is, in short, a book about who controls 'reality' and how, and about the plight of individuals who struggle against the odds to discover their authentic selves and to avoid being passively constituted by the customs, language and social pressures around them. The book models a situation; it is up to the reader how that model is applied. Orwell himself disliked

CHECK THE FILM

In Michael Radford's film *1984* (1984), Party members salute by raising their arms, crossed at the wrists with fists clenched. This gives them an appearance of being handcuffed, **symbolising** that they are under the control of Big Brother.

homosexuality, for example, but it is perfectly possible that there are homosexuals who might feel that Winston speaks for them too.

No amount of relevance could preserve *Nineteen Eighty-Four* as a classic, however, if it did not also have strong artistic merits. The majority of readers have experienced it as a masterpiece of political insight and literary clarity, but there has always been a small but determined minority who dismiss it as crude and unconvincing propaganda. It is true that it contains **stereotypical** characters, melodramatic episodes and long passages of discussion. However, a **science fiction dystopia** is no more to be judged on its **characterisation** and unobtrusive exposition than a **realistic** novel is to be judged on its sociopolitical ideas and its success in making fantastic events seem plausible. For the kind of book it is, *Nineteen Eighty-Four* is clearly very good indeed. There have been thousands of stories about the future published since it appeared, but none have had anything like the same impact, because none of them have combined the familiar and the fantastic in a way so alarmingly believable or devised a form which conveys that fearsome vision so intensely. Putting us into Winston's head and, still more unnervingly, into his frail and vulnerable body, Orwell lets us experience his frustration, rebellion and final defeat in a way which is impossible to forget.

www. CHECK THE NET
Search an online encyclopedia such as **http://en. wikipedia.org** for excellent information, resources and links on Orwell.

The world of Winston Smith has become a significant part of modern folklore. At the time these Notes were written, there were television series in Britain entitled *Big Brother* and *Room 101*. Their makers could safely assume that viewers would understand the references, even if they had not read the book. However, the naming of TV shows is hardly a tribute which the inventor of the telescreen would have valued and is parasitic upon a far more impressive achievement of *Nineteen Eighty-Four*, which is that it has given us a language for naming threats to our freedom. Time and again the words 'Orwellian', 'Doublethink' and 'Big Brother' have been used to attack and discredit proposals or developments which seem to lead us towards the closed, hate-filled world which Orwell depicted. He imagined his worst fears so powerfully precisely because he wanted to make it as difficult as he could for them to come true, and in this he undoubtedly succeeded.

It is just possible that in the twenty-first century we may come to live in a world so unlike Winston's that his sufferings will be virtually unintelligible to us, but it is not likely. In the final analysis *Nineteen Eighty-Four* is not about 1948 or 1984, but about the human condition. It is a book with a limited vision perhaps, but an intense one, and it conveys it so well that it is likely to remain a classic, whatever the future brings.

 **QUESTION**

In your view, has the passing of the year 1984 made the novel *Nineteen Eighty-Four* any less significant?

PART TWO

THE TEXT

NOTE ON THE TEXT

Nineteen Eighty-Four was first published in 1949 by Secker & Warburg, London. The most fully annotated edition of the book is the one edited by Orwell's biographer, Bernard Crick, published in 1984 by the Clarendon Press, Oxford.

CHECK THE NET

You can search the text of *Nineteen Eighty-Four* for key words at **http://www.online-literature.com**

In 1987 an edition edited by Peter Davison was published by Secker & Warburg as Volume 9 of the *Complete Works of George Orwell*. It was based on Orwell's typescript of November 1948, amended to include proof corrections from the first British and American editions. This text was reprinted in 1989, with an introduction by Ben Pimlott, as a paperback Penguin Twentieth-Century Classic. All the references in the present study are to this paperback edition of the 'authoritative' text.

SYNOPSIS

In a year which is called '1984', an elite known as the Party controls all aspects of life in Britain, which is now named Airstrip One and incorporated into the superstate of Oceania. Winston Smith, a minor member of the Party, works at the so-called Ministry of Truth, rewriting records of the past in order to make them conform to the official version of events. However, while outwardly acting in accordance with the Party's requirements, Winston dreams of the past and of a landscape which he thinks of as the 'Golden Country'. He starts to keep a secret diary of his thoughts, speculating, for example, whether the lower-class 'proles' might ever overthrow the Party, and recalls one occasion when he had physical proof that the Party's account of past events was untrue. In the slums of north London Winston tries unsuccessfully to learn something of the past from an elderly prole in a pub. He then returns to the junk shop where he bought his diary and purchases a coral paperweight which becomes for him a symbol of the lost past and of life outside government control.

One day he is shocked to receive a love note from a girl called Julia, whom he has previously suspected of spying on him for the Thought Police. The two arrange to meet secretly in the countryside and they begin an affair, an act of political rebellion because it places physical desire above Party discipline. In order that he and Julia can spend more time together, Winston rents a room above the junk shop. O'Brien, an apparently dissident member of the Inner Party, invites the couple to become members of a secret revolutionary organisation known as the Brotherhood.

After many years of war with Eurasia, Oceania suddenly goes to war against Eastasia, taking Eurasia for its ally. In order to make the Party's policies seem consistent, employees at the Ministry of Truth have to work overtime to revise all the materials which have ever indicated the contrary. Once this is done, Winston returns to the room above the junk shop, meets up with Julia and begins to read the Brotherhood's secret book. Before he can finish it, however, the Thought Police burst into the room and take the couple prisoner.

In the cells of the Ministry of Love, Winston meets other people who have been arrested, including several of his colleagues. Eventually he discovers that O'Brien is not a dissident, but a member of the Thought Police who has lured him into a trap. O'Brien now uses a combination of reason, torture and drugs to persuade Winston that whatever the Party states to be true must be so. Under this pressure, Winston tries to accept the mentality that the Party demands of him, but cannot entirely lose his old emotions. His love still belongs to Julia, not to the Party's leader, Big Brother. When Winston cries out to Julia in a dream, O'Brien decides it is time to send him to Room 101, the place where prisoners are confronted with their worst fears. Here Winston's face is attached to a cage full of rats. He screams for the pain to be applied to Julia instead of to him. After his resulting breakdown and 'conversion', Winston becomes one of the former 'traitors' who drink at the Chestnut Tree Café while awaiting their eventual execution. He reflects on his past and future and he listens to news of a military victory. He now has no feelings of hostility to the system. Instead, he loves Big Brother.

CONTEXT

Winston's problem in distinguishing between rebels and double agents has many historic parallels. Orwell's own anti-Soviet book *Animal Farm* (1945) was apparently turned down by one publisher on the advice of a senior official at the Ministry of Information who is now known to have been a Soviet spy. More recently, after the collapse of the East European Communist regimes in 1989, official records revealed that some highly respected people had been secret police informers.

DETAILED SUMMARIES

PART ONE

CHAPTER 1

- Winston Smith, a citizen of a state where the government controls all aspects of life, starts keeping a secret diary of his thoughts.

3 **fruity** sounding rich, drawling and upper class in quality

4 **Three-Year Plan** the term recalls the Five-Year Plans for economic development produced by the Communist government in the USSR from 1928 onwards

5 **baulks** squared lengths of wood

7 **quarto-sized** roughly nine by eleven inches

17 **like Saint Sebastian** the death of Saint Sebastian, a Roman Christian of the third century, is the subject of many paintings

Winston Smith returns from work at the Ministry of Truth to his flat in Victory Mansions, London, passing a poster of the Party leader bearing the slogan 'Big Brother is watching you' (p. 3). Other indications of the state's far-reaching power are evident, such as the Party uniform which Winston wears and the compulsory 'telescreen' in his flat. This device not only broadcasts propaganda but is also used by the 'Thought Police' to monitor its viewers' activities. Britain (which is now known as Airstrip One and is a province of a superstate called Oceania) is involved in a war with the superstate of Eurasia and is allied to Eastasia. In the past the allegiance has sometimes been the other way around, but this is never admitted.

The long-term impact of the conflict can be seen in bomb sites, rationing and a powerful Ministry of Peace which is responsible for running the war. The Ministry of Truth, where Winston works, controls news, education and cultural activities. There are also Ministries of Plenty (economic affairs) and Love (law and order), the latter a fiercely guarded fortress. Winston struggles to recall whether life in London was different from this in his childhood, but he is unable to remember. He cannot even be sure of the date – supposedly 4 April 1984 – since so much of the information propagated by the state is false.

Winston's living room has a slightly unusual design which enables him to move out of sight of the telescreen. Placing himself in an alcove, he takes out a beautiful old book which he has bought in a junk shop and starts to write in it a diary of his thoughts, an act which he knows is likely to lead to his execution since thinking for oneself is now forbidden as 'thoughtcrime'. He writes firstly about an incident at a cinema the previous night when a lower-class woman (a 'prole') objected to the violent content of a war film; he then breaks off to reflect on an incident at work which he believes is what prompted him at last to begin writing the diary.

He was taking part in the 'Two Minutes Hate', a ritual during which images of the state's chief enemy, Emmanuel Goldstein, are displayed on the telescreens. Goldstein is seen advocating freedom of speech and assembly, and crying out that the Revolution has been betrayed. The viewers experience a frenzy of hatred for him and love of Big Brother. The broadcast ends with the three Party slogans: 'War is Peace', 'Freedom is Slavery', 'Ignorance is Strength' (p. 18). Winston had reacted strongly to two other people who were present at this particular Two Minutes Hate. One was a young woman from the Fiction Department, where novels are written by machines. He hates her because, although she is attractive, she seems to be dedicated to the Party, which tries to repress its members' sexual feelings. The other is a member of the Inner Party, named O'Brien, with whom Winston feels a mysterious affinity and whose expression on this occasion he takes to be a sign of encouragement. While he is recalling the Two Minutes Hate, Winston unconsciously writes *DOWN WITH BIG BROTHER* in the book several times (p. 20). He feels alarmed at this, but reflects that whatever he does the outcome will be the same. Sooner or later he is certain to be executed for thoughtcrime. Even as he is thinking this, a knock comes at the door.

COMMENTARY

The book's opening unobtrusively conveys a considerable amount of information, as well as involving us deeply in the story. By the end of the first page, we have a clear idea of the world in which Winston lives, with its sordid living conditions and fierce government controls. By the time we reach the end of the chapter, we have been introduced to the three principal characters and most of the main features of their society. We also have a good notion of the book's themes and even its outcome. We are, moreover, caught

CHECK THE FILM

Because a film has to be visually dramatic and cannot enter a character's thoughts in the direct way that a novel can, Michael Radford's *1984* (1984) does not open with Winston beginning his diary, but with the Two Minutes Hate. Later on, voice-overs give us occasional glimpses of Winston's thoughts.

up in the drama of Winston's situation and anxious about who is at the door.

The **characterisation** of Julia (the girl, unnamed at this stage) and O'Brien is simple but effective. Orwell gives us a sketch of their appearance and mannerisms, followed by a summary of Winston's feelings about them. Winston himself is a more elaborate creation. While we sympathise with his rebellion, we also notice that he has not yet had the chance to fully develop his own point of view. He lapses back into the standard Party attitude when writing about the prole woman at the cinema. Indeed, throughout the chapter he **stereotypes** women and expresses hatred and contempt for them. His condition seems to be **symbolised** by the ulcer above his right ankle. Mentally and physically malnourished, he aspires to health. If his views are not always true, he is nonetheless fighting to escape from a system of ideas which is thoroughly wicked. The book starts at a decisive moment in this struggle, the opening of the diary. Writing the diary is a way of creating a mental space outside the regulated world of Big Brother where Winston can start to explore and develop his own feelings and ideas.

 QUESTION

What narrative techniques does Orwell use in telling the story of *Nineteen Eighty-Four,* and how successful do you judge them to be?

Although this story is focused on Winston, it is narrated in the third person, using **free indirect discourse**. That is to say, we see events from Winston's viewpoint and many sentences seem to echo his thoughts, but the 'voice' we hear is not his but that of a narrator. For example, the references to 'an eighteenth-century nobleman' (p. 12) and 'Saint Sebastian' (p. 17) are unlikely to come from Winston's own knowledge. The narrator's presence **distances** us slightly from Winston's standpoint, discouraging us from completely identifying with him. At the same time, free indirect discourse also helps Orwell to integrate action, ideas and characterisation into a single story. Rather than just being given information about the Two Minutes Hate, for example, we are able to track Winston's changing feelings and thoughts and become involved in them.

The world which the book depicts is a speculative, **science fictional** one, but is firmly rooted in the first half of the twentieth century and contains many references to which readers in Orwell's day would have had an immediate response. The poster of Big Brother, for example, recalls the familiar recruitment poster of 1914 on which Lord Kitchener, the Secretary of War, declared 'Your Country needs YOU'. The Two Minutes Hate seems to be a distasteful inversion of the Two Minutes Silence, held annually on 11 November to show respect for those killed in the World Wars. The descriptions of London in the opening pages of the book are highly reminiscent of the late 1940s, with bomb sites, power cuts, economy drives and paternalistic propaganda. (For possible references to political issues of the period, see **Social and political background**.) It has even been suggested by some people that the Ministry of Truth is meant to resemble in its appearance, if not in its size, Senate House at the University of London, where the Ministry of Information was housed during the Second World War. This ministry was indirectly responsible for censoring Orwell's work as a broadcaster. Its telegraphic address was 'Miniform' and the Minister himself, Brendan Bracken, was sometimes known to his subordinates as 'BB'.

The predominant mood of the opening chapter seems a fearful one, but we should not overlook an admixture of **satirical comedy**. The effect of the gin on Winston ('one had the sensation of being hit on the back of the head with a rubber club', p. 7) is grimly humorous, and there is tongue-in-cheek satire in the novel-writing machines, which make fun of popular fiction for its clichés; the telescreens, which mock the resumption of television after the war; and the Two Minutes Hate, which **caricatures** religious and political fanaticism.

Despite its resemblances to the world of 1948, Orwell establishes right away that the world of '1984' is a strange and sinister one by having the clocks strike thirteen, a number traditionally associated with bad fortune. Modern readers may not find the twenty-four-hour clock a chilling innovation, nor the use of metric measurements which are emphasised throughout the book, but it is likely that the original readers would have found both these systems of reckoning disturbingly alien. While most European countries 'went metric' in the 1830s, it was not until the 1970s that the use of decimal-based measurement became at all widespread in Britain (to be established for many purposes, appropriately enough, by the

CONTEXT

When the book first appeared, the printers of the American edition were so puzzled by the metric measurements that they tried to convert them into feet and inches.

middle of the 1980s). More unsettling even than the rationalisation of traditional measurement is the rationalisation of traditional sovereignty, with Britain absorbed into a superstate dominated by the USA and no longer important in its own right, only for its military value as 'Airstrip One'. This is another piece of satire, this time on Britain's changing place in the international order.

There is much going on in the first chapter, then – more than may at first be apparent – but the information is arranged so skilfully that it is all easily absorbed. The reader is not confused but intrigued, though the source of suspense is not so much what is going to happen (Winston firmly expects to be arrested and 'vaporized') as exactly when and how it will occur. We may wonder what part the girl and O'Brien will play in the process. For a suspicious reader, or a person reading the book for the second time, perhaps the most intriguing question is whether Winston is being 'set up'. Is it really an accident that there is a place in his flat where he cannot be seen by the telescreen, or has he been allocated the flat precisely so that his loyalty can be tested?

CHAPTER 2

- Winston helps a neighbour, Mrs Parsons.
- He silently reflects on the futility of his private act of rebellion.

The person knocking at Winston's door proves to be his neighbour, Mrs Parsons, who asks him to unblock her kitchen sink. While helping her, he thinks about her husband, Tom, who is an enthusiastic supporter of the ruling Party, and their children, an unruly boy and girl who terrorise their mother and who, Winston speculates, may one day denounce her to the state for some supposed deviation from orthodoxy. The children are particularly restless today because it has not been possible for them to go to the public hanging of some Eurasian prisoners, supposedly guilty of war crimes. As Winston leaves, the boy fires a catapult at him and calls him Goldstein.

Returning to his flat, Winston recalls a strange dream in which a voice which he later identified as O'Brien's said to him, 'We shall meet in the place where there is no darkness' (p. 27). He cannot be sure whether O'Brien is a friend or enemy, and he is not even sure that it matters so long as O'Brien is someone who understands his feelings. Winston hears a report on the telescreen that the chocolate ration has been reduced, accompanied by a counterbalancing claim of military victory, and reflects on the difficulty of knowing anything beyond the state's propaganda. The system is enforced through the 'sacred principles' of 'Ingsoc'. These principles are 'Newspeak' (the development of a simplified language which makes it hard to think unorthodox thoughts), 'doublethink' (holding to an official belief while acting on a more realistic unofficial one which contradicts it) and 'the mutability of the past' (believing that it is possible to change history by rewriting it). The state seems all-powerful and Winston's diary-writing futile. Nonetheless, he writes another entry and conceals his diary in a drawer.

COMMENTARY

We see how much Winston values the diary by his refusal to close it for fear of smudging what he has written, even though this leaves his 'thoughtcrime' wide open to detection. Our suspense is relieved when we discover that the caller is not after all a member of the Thought Police, but Mrs Parsons, a stereotypical downtrodden housewife. She and her family contrast with Winston in their orthodoxy and also demonstrate the squalid horror of life under Big Brother. We are given firm opinions about them – Parsons, for instance, is a 'man of paralysing stupidity' (p. 24) – which presumably reflect Winston's thoughts. We may well accept these judgements uncritically and perhaps find some humour in grotesque details like the dust in the creases of Mrs Parsons's face But should we go on accepting them when Winston reflects that a 'nosing zealot ... a woman, probably' (p. 30) might detect evidence of his diary writings? Some critics have judged that contempt for women is so deeply engrained in the book that misogyny is a characteristic not just of Winston, but of the text itself.

The Parsonses' children, corrupted by the state into bullying spies, demonstrate that life in '1984' is not only squalid but sinister. It

CONTEXT

The Spies, the Youth League and the Junior Anti-Sex League are **satirical** equivalents to the Hitler Youth in Germany and the Komsomol in Soviet Russia. In Nazi Germany children were sometimes taken away and placed in foster homes if their parents refused to enrol them in the Hitler Youth.

becomes altogether nightmarish when we read of Winston's strange dreams. His sense of reality seems to be under attack both from without (the state's intrusions and propaganda) and from within (his dreams) and, eerily, the dreams seem to have begun coming true, with O'Brien now identified as the owner of the mysterious voice.

CHAPTER 3

- Winston conforms outwardly to the Party's routines, waking and exercising in time to orders from the telescreen.
- However, his dreams and thoughts are of the past and of the 'Golden Country', a pastoral landscape to which his mind often returns.

Winston dreams of the death of his mother and sister, whom he pictures looking up at him from inside a sinking ship. He conceives of his mother's death as a self-sacrifice on his behalf, and feels that it was tragic in a way that is now no longer possible because private motivations such as family loyalty have been destroyed by the state. Next, he has a contrasting dream of being in the countryside on a sunny day (in what in his waking hours he thinks of as 'the Golden Country', p. 33), watching the girl from the Fiction Department walk towards him, taking off her clothes. His sleep is broken by a morning alarm whistle from the telescreen, followed by a programme of compulsory physical exercises. While he executes these, Winston again struggles to recall details of his childhood, particularly his experience of an air raid, and reflects upon the way that events since then have been distorted. Oceania is supposed to have been at war with Eurasia and allied to Eastasia for a long period, but Winston knows that four years ago Eastasia was the enemy and Eurasia the ally. Similarly, Big Brother's leadership of the Party has been backdated by decades and the Party falsely credits itself with the invention of the aeroplane. Winston's reverie is interrupted by the instructor on the telescreen, who singles him out so aggressively for slacking that for once he does succeed in touching his toes.

CONTEXT

At the time Orwell was writing the book, in the years 1947 to 1948, Britain was an ally of the US superstate and faced the possibility of war with its former ally, the Russian superstate. Cities like London were full of bomb sites. Rationing was in force, run by a government whose ministries exercised strong control over everyday life.

COMMENTARY

The first two chapters have introduced us to Winston at the decisive moment when his thoughts pass from dissatisfaction to rebellion. The remainder of Part One contains little **plot** development, but instead deepens our knowledge of Winston and the world in which he is trapped. We follow him through episodes from a typical day and watch him making entries in his diary. Through both situations we learn about the world in which he lives and we also share his thoughts, feelings and memories.

Chapter 3 contains much information about life in '1984', including the inaccurate, **stereotypical** history taught to schoolchildren and the morning exercises which are compulsory for Party members (**parodying** the exercises which in the 1940s the BBC broadcast before the seven o'clock news), but there is a greater emphasis than previously on Winston's inner life. The **image** of his mother and sister trapped in the sinking ship is an emotionally disturbing one. Their self-sacrifice contrasts with what is to happen in Part Three, Chapter 5, when Winston has to make a choice of whether to sacrifice himself or another. As an epitome of entrapment and death (repeated in Part One, Chapter 7, to describe the proles), the image of the sinking ship also contrasts with Winston's dream of the Golden Country, though in turn the natural imagery of both makes a contrast with the man-made world of '1984'. The way the waking world and Winston's dreams **dissolve** into one another recalls the editing style of the film shown during the Two Minutes Hate and probably reflects the influence of cinema on Orwell's writing. (He had reviewed films for the magazine *Time and Tide* in 1940 and 1941.)

Why does Winston wake with the word 'Shakespeare' on his lips? It is probably because Shakespeare's work depicts a more natural world than the one in which Winston lives, a world containing rounded characters capable of surprising us with their behaviour and of experiencing **tragedy**. In Winston's world people are too limited in their ideas and actions to achieve tragic status, and the natural has systematically been replaced by the artificial, as O'Brien boasts in Part Three, Chapter 3. We cannot therefore expect Winston to develop into a tragic hero like Othello or Hamlet,

? QUESTION

What are the effects of the first-person narrative on the reader? What might have been gained or lost if the book had been written in the third person?

CHECK THE BOOK

There is a detailed discussion of the Shakespeare references used by Huxley in the York Notes Advanced guide to *Brave New World*.

making powerful speeches full of insights into the human condition. His death cannot leave us impressed by the folly and the grandeur of the soul. He is merely one victim among millions, struggling to understand the processes which are destroying the residual sense of humanity he possesses. The reference to Shakespeare is reminiscent of Aldous Huxley's 1932 **dystopia** *Brave New World* (see **Literary background**) in which John the Savage repeatedly attacks the World State of the future by quoting from Shakespeare's works. However, Orwell's attempt to revive the device is too abrupt and unexplained to be comparably effective.

CHAPTER 4

• Winston works at the Ministry of Truth, rewriting items in the *Times* in order to make them conform to later developments.

Winston's job at the so-called Ministry of Truth is to rewrite past issues of the *Times* in order to bring them into line with the most recent version of history approved by the Party. All records, from novels to cartoons, have to be falsified in this way. Elsewhere in the building, newspapers, literature, pornography and popular songs are being produced to meet the Party's requirements, ensuring that all sections of the population receive only the ideas and information which the Party authorises.

Changes have to be made today to a prediction about military events, to a forecast about production figures and to a pledge to increase the chocolate ration, which now becomes a warning that the ration may have to be reduced. Winston's most challenging task, however, is to rewrite a speech in which Big Brother has awarded decorations to a Comrade Withers. Withers has since become an 'unperson', probably executed, with all evidence of his existence destroyed. Winston decides to transfer the decoration to an entirely imaginary hero, Comrade Ogilvy, and invents a suitably virtuous life for him.

COMMENTARY

This rewriting of the truth carries conviction, no doubt due to Orwell's own experiences in wartime radio and his wife's in the government's Censorship Department (see **Background: George Orwell**). The government made much use of such falsification in the Second World War, both to boost Allied morale and to mislead the enemy. The technique is now universal and is known as 'disinformation' – appropriately, a word made in the Newspeak fashion by adding a prefix to an existing word. It is **ironic** to find that Winston is skilled in concocting elaborate items of disinformation, when we have previously seen him reduced to semi-literacy trying to write his diary. The problems he experiences in expressing his personal thoughts are not, it is clear, caused by lack of ability, only by a lifetime's lack of practice.

The biography Winston invents for Ogilvy is probably no great exaggeration of the deeds attributed to heroes in totalitarian societies. However, most readers will find it ridiculous and it is an interesting question whether Winston's bosses would have had a similar reaction, since a suspicion of insincerity and **parody** in his writing would surely be enough to attract the attention of the Thought Police.

The churning out of inferior journalism, entertainment and art by the Ministry in order to keep the population in a condition of mental slavery **satirises** propaganda of all kinds. Although Orwell certainly has in mind the distortion of news practised by Communist Russia and Nazi Germany, his ridicule is more wide ranging. The co-opting of creativity for propaganda was a general feature of the arts in wartime Britain, and of the kind of crude political writing which Orwell attacked in essays like 'The Prevention of Literature' (1946). Comrade Ogilvy's life also recalls the virtuous deeds which churches sometimes attribute to saints. If there is an element of **comic** parody in this satire, the erasure of Comrade Withers brings a more chilling note into the chapter, as his is a fate which Winston must expect to share.

CONTEXT

The Times, a leading British newspaper since the late eighteenth century, and long regarded as a national newspaper of record (i.e. a reliable archive of information), was also noted in Orwell's day for its right-of-centre views and pre-war advocacy of appeasement towards the Nazis.

CONTEXT

In 1947, when Orwell was writing the book, the British sweet ration was raised from four to five ounces per week, but the tinned meat ration was cut to twopence-worth per week due to an economy drive.

 CHECK THE BOOK

Orwell's essay 'The Prevention of Literature' is included in *Essays* (1994) and other collections of his writings.

GLOSSARY

51 **philologist** an expert on the history of language

52 **flicks** cinema

CHECK THE BOOK

Orwell's own views on language, very unlike those of Syme, may be found in his essay 'Politics and the English Language', which is included in *Essays* (1994) and other collections of his writings.

CHAPTER 5

- Over lunch, Winston talks with two colleagues whose conformity depresses him.
- He suspects that he is being spied on by another of them, the girl from the Fiction Department.

Winston spends his lunchtime in the Ministry canteen with Syme, a colleague who is working on the Eleventh Edition of the Newspeak Dictionary. Syme enthuses about how thoroughly he and his colleagues are reducing the English vocabulary. Soon people's capacity to think unorthodox thoughts will be inhibited because they will not have the words needed to formulate them. As he listens, Winston suspects that Syme is too clever and indiscreet for his own good and that he will one day be killed by the Party. While the two men are talking, they are joined by Parsons, who boasts of how his daughter and her friends followed a stranger and denounced him as a spy, possibly resulting in the man's execution. Winston reflects that Parsons, in contrast to Syme, will never be vaporised by the state because he is so uncritically enthusiastic about its policies. Together they listen to a series of announcements from the Ministry of Plenty, and Winston is depressed by the way the others seem to effortlessly believe the lies that they hear. He is also alarmed by the sight of the girl from the Fiction Department, who seems to be following him. He fears she is spying on him with the intention of denouncing him to the Thought Police.

COMMENTARY

We continue to track Winston through a typical day, observing life in '1984' and at the same time overhearing his secret thoughts of dissent. Syme and Parsons are brought into the story for a number of reasons. As additional characters, they add solidity to the world described. They and their ideas are also established here so that they can be dramatically reintroduced later. (Syme's reference to the Chestnut Tree Café looks ahead to Part One, Chapter 7 and to Part Three, Chapter 6. Parsons's praise of his children's spying has an **ironic** outcome in Part Three, Chapter 1.) Syme clarifies the significance of Newspeak, while he and Parsons exemplify the mentality and the beliefs of Party members. Their open callousness concerning executions may seem excessive, particularly Syme's sadistic relish at a hanging, but such views are ones easily held about enemies in wartime and the Party has worked hard to build up all that is worst in human nature. Although Orwell himself had killed people in battle, he was shocked by casual references to murder in films, novels and poems and repeatedly attacked such attitudes as morally ignorant, for example in his essays 'Inside the Whale' (1940) and 'Raffles and Miss Blandish' (1944).

 CHECK THE BOOK
'Inside the Whale' and 'Raffles and Miss Blandish' can be found in *Essays* (1994) and other collections of Orwell's writings.

CHAPTER 6

- Winston uses his diary to record a visit he made to a prostitute three years ago.
- He reflects on how the Party has perverted people's natural sexual feelings.

Winston records in his diary a visit he made to a prostitute three years previously. While writing down his experiences, he recalls how he separated from his wife Katharine a decade ago, partly because, as a good Party member, she regarded sex as a pleasureless duty to be gone through in order to create a child. Winston longs for a healthy sexual relationship and regards such expedients as his visit to the ageing prostitute with horror.

COMMENTARY

We begin with another diary entry, although 'diary' is really a misnomer since by this stage most of what Winston writes either concerns events long past or takes the form of general reflections. As he struggles to set down on paper the aspects of life which most disturb him, the movement between present thoughts, memories of past occurrences and general philosophising helps maintain pace and interest, involving us in Winston's struggle to discover himself. The Party's repression of knowledge includes self-knowledge and this has psychological consequences for the citizens of Oceania, as we see in Winston's dreams and longings. His rebellion is a political one, but it also has a psychological dimension.

In its hostility to and regulation of sex, the Party resembles any number of societies, and any number of religions and political organisations within them, but the Party consciously takes control over people to an extreme. The sexual frustration depicted here goes some way towards explaining Winston's misogyny and perhaps also accounts for some of the motivation behind his rebellion. However, we might wish to hear Katharine's side of the story and even the prostitute's. Both of them are such **stereotypical** figures that we are entitled to question whether Winston is sufficiently detached to give us a full view of the world he is describing.

(See **Text 1** of **Extended commentaries** for a more detailed discussion of part of this chapter.)

GLOSSARY

76 *jus primae noctis* an alleged custom by which a lord might have sex with the bride of one of his tenants on their wedding night. If it ever existed, however, it was in the medieval period, not the era of industrial capitalism

CHAPTER 7

- Continuing his diary entries, Winston speculates whether the proles could ever overthrow the Party, recalls one occasion when he had physical proof that the Party's account of events is untrue and wonders what motivates the Party to maintain its hold on reality.
- Finally, he decides that O'Brien is the ideal reader for his thoughts.

Winston's thoughts turn to the proles, who form eighty-five per cent of the population. Of all the elements of society, only they have the physical strength to overthrow the Party, but they are preoccupied with the hard lives they lead and with the distractions which the state offers them, such as gambling on the lottery. Winston again reflects on the impossibility facing even an educated person like himself in learning what life was like before the Revolution. He can see the discrepancy between the Party's claims about society and the drab reality he experiences, and he is sure that much that appears in the history books is untrue, but the evidence has all been doctored by people like himself. Only once did he have actual proof of the state's lies. The document concerned three 'traitors' whom he saw in the late '1960s' at the Chestnut Tree Café, passing the time until their eventual execution by drinking gin and listening to a telescreen jeeringly sing, 'Under the spreading chestnut tree / I sold you and you sold me' (p. 80). In '1973', while working on some documents, he came across a photograph torn out of the *Times*, showing the three men together in New York. This contradicted statements in their confessions that on the date in question they were in Eurasia. Winston could not show this evidence to anyone, and destroyed it after about ten minutes to avoid incrimination.

 QUESTION
Winston has problems learning about the past. How do we know about history? How reliable or representative is the information and the interpretations of it which you can find today? How do you know?

Even after many years of reflection, he cannot understand why the Party shapes society as it does and he feels in despair at this, but he takes courage from the thought that O'Brien may be on his side. Thinking of him as his reader, he concludes the diary entry by stating: 'Freedom is the freedom to say that two plus two makes four. If that is granted, all else follows' (p. 84).

COMMENTARY

Again we start with the diary, through which we continue to learn both about life in '1984' and about Winston. The fate of the three 'traitors' reminds us of the penalty he might have to undergo for his own small rebellion. Given the ominous reputation of the café, we may wonder why Winston was near it, risking attracting the attention of the Thought Police. It never seems to occur to him that the picture of the three men might have been sent in order to test his reaction, but this may well be the case, especially since it is so readily produced again in Part Three, Chapter 2.

Winston's proposition that 'Freedom is the freedom to say that two plus two makes four' is a key idea in the book, taken up at greater length in Part Three. It expresses memorably the idea that our surest knowledge of what is real comes from the evidence of our senses, a philosophical position known as 'empiricism'. Winston puts forward this empiricist view, yet he is haunted by the fear that the Party can control all the evidence available to the senses and so in effect change reality. Furthermore, in his own experience, the world he perceives through his senses is oddly mixed up with the world of his dreams. Because of all this, Winston longs to find someone whose judgement he respects, someone who can, almost like a substitute for God, assure him that his view of life is the correct one. He decides that O'Brien is such an authority figure.

The only hope of actually overthrowing the Party, Winston believes, lies in the proles. However, from the evidence we are given, it seems a very poor hope. In the opening pages of the chapter we are told that the proles are 'like animals', 'like cattle' (p. 74) and, if they were to rebel, it would be 'like a horse shaking off flies' (p. 73), an **image** reminiscent of Boxer, the carthorse who **symbolises** the working class in Orwell's book *Animal Farm* (1945). A criticism frequently made of *Animal Farm* is that, by creating a **fable** in which people are represented by farm animals, Orwell patronises people and **stereotypes** them as natural victims. The same may be said of the proles, who are, we should remember, eighty-five per cent of the nation. Even on the most pessimistic assessment of human society, this seems an extraordinarily large section of the population to be so ignorant and passive. It would certainly include most readers of these Notes, for example. Many critics have suggested that Orwell found it difficult to accurately perceive those below him in the class structure, even though he was trying to rebel against his elite background. However, we should also remember that Winston is not entirely reliable in his views. At times his judgements and predictions prove faulty. Although when we look through his eyes we see a lone rebel fighting an unshakeable system, there is some evidence as the story unfolds that the system is not as secure as it claims, and even at the end of the book the question of how widespread resistance might be remains an open one. Perhaps we should not take Winston's view of the proles and the power of the Party at face value, but should instead realise how difficult it is for a Party member like him to see the world clearly.

CHECK THE BOOK

Animal Farm (1945), Orwell's satire on the Russian Revolution, was the book that made him famous.

CHECK THE BOOK

Orwell's views on the working classes are discussed most explicitly in his book *The Road to Wigan Pier* (1937).

CHAPTER 8

- Winston wanders in the slums of north London and tries unsuccessfully to learn something of the past from an elderly prole in a pub.

- He then returns to the junk shop where he bought the diary and purchases a coral paperweight.

- On his way home, he once again sees the girl from the Fiction Department and is more than ever convinced that she is spying on him.

Winston truants from an evening at the Community Centre and wanders instead through the slums of north London, observing and reflecting upon the proles. After escaping death from a rocket bomb, he enters a pub and strikes up a conversation with an elderly man, hoping that his informant will be able to give him a first-hand account of the past. However, the information he receives is so fragmentary and personal as to be useless. Winston leaves the pub and wanders the streets until he finds himself at the junk shop where he bought the diary. Here he buys a beautiful coral paperweight and talks to the shop owner, Charrington, about various relics of the past, including the nursery rhyme 'Oranges and lemons'. On his way home he is terrified to find himself passing the girl from the Fiction Department. He now believes more than ever that she is spying on him and will soon denounce him to the authorities.

COMMENTARY

In the first part of the chapter we witness Winston's unsuccessful attempts to make contact with the proles. The way he kicks aside a dead prole's hand shows that he has not yet learned to regard the lower class as fellow human beings and his cross-purpose conversation with the old man in the pub **comically** demonstrates the gulf between his ideas and theirs. As a **satire** on the distance between radical intellectuals and the so-called masses, the episode is certainly effective. Nonetheless, almost all commentators on the book agree that the representation of the proles remains a problem.

QUESTION

How credible do you find Orwell's depiction of the proles?

Their speech and behaviour is **stereotypical** and unconvincing, encouraging us to accept Winston's negative evaluation of them. At the same time, the old man's speech, with its dismissive remarks about women, even though it is intended to be amusing, tends to reinforce the somewhat hostile view of women already taken by Winston. When we are told that Charrington's accent is 'less debased than that of the majority of proles' (p. 98) the word 'debased' suggests that an accent like Winston's, one spoken by an educated minority, is not just more respectable than other people's but more correct, and that the accent of the majority of speakers is a corrupted version of it. Winston may well have been taught this false linguistic history, but is it also the narrator's view and are we supposed to share it? When Winston enters the world of the proles, he seems to be entering a world of stereotypes, more likely to confirm readers' prejudices than to help us see class and gender conflict more clearly.

Charrington's accent has an additional significance because it is a clue that he is not really a prole. Since he was the one who sold Winston the diary and who offers him a private room to rent, we are again confronted with the question of how much of Winston's rebellion is actually a trap set up for him by others. Surprisingly few commentators have suggested that the girl, Julia, might be a member of the Thought Police, as Winston at first suspected, but surely it is suspicious that he notices her following him when he leaves the shop and that she appears on the scene immediately after he has been shown the room.

The chapter ends with Winston's fear that the girl is about to denounce him, with the powerful description of his physical vulnerability to torture and with the riddling Party slogans. The slogans of the Party and Winston's dreams have both been established as **motifs** which, as they are repeated, help to shape the story. In this chapter they are joined by two more: the paperweight and the mysterious nursery rhyme 'Oranges and lemons'.

PART TWO

CHAPTER 1

- The girl from the Fiction Department passes Winston a love note.
- They arrange to meet secretly in the countryside.

Winston again sees the girl from the Fiction Department, this time at work. She has one arm in a sling and, as they pass, she falls. He is surprised to find how much he sympathises with her, and even more surprised when she takes advantage of his concern to secretly pass him a piece of paper. He wonders anxiously whether the message could be from the Thought Police or perhaps from the Brotherhood, a conspiracy to overthrow the Party of which he has heard rumours. After allowing several minutes to pass, he reads the paper and is stunned to find the message, '*I love you*' (p. 113).

COMMENTARY

Winston lives in inner turmoil for over a week until he has an opportunity to make contact with the girl in the Ministry canteen. They arrange to meet in Victory Square. When they do so, she gives him instructions for a rendezvous in the countryside the following Sunday.

Like the first part of the book, Part Two begins at a decisive moment, in this case the morning when Winston receives the note from Julia. Now that there is more action in the story, there are fewer references to Winston's diary and virtually all the chapters in this section of the book begin, not with Winston's reflections, but by dropping the reader straight into the action.

Orwell's skills as a storyteller are evident throughout the chapter. The delay between Winston receiving the note and finding the opportunity to read it is used to build suspense. He finally reads it in the same circumstances in which he read the article about the three 'traitors' in Part One, Chapter 7, suggesting its equivalent

QUESTION

How does Orwell's use of language contribute to the effectiveness of the novel?

? QUESTION

How far does
Orwell succeed
in making the
relationship
between Winston
and Julia a
plausible and
moving one?

importance. After all the propaganda and verbal manipulation we
have encountered previously in the book, Julia's message stands out
as a simple subject-verb-object statement of emotion, '*I love you*'.

Like Winston, we are eager for the two to meet and we share his
impatience at the obstacles in their way, not least the man who
almost takes the empty place at her table. The text never tells us
explicitly that Winston tripped him up, so we share the initial
confusion of the other people in the canteen, even though we
quickly conclude that he must have done so. Sighting the poet
Ampleforth not only prompts Winston to speak to Julia, it also
reminds us of Ampleforth's existence, so that we will remember him
when he is reintroduced in Part Three, Chapter 1. When Winston
and Julia do speak, their conversation is terse, made up of short
sentences without any reporting clauses (such as 'she said'), making
it very clear how guarded their conversation has to be. Finally, the
tryst in Victory Square is visually **symbolic** of their relationship.
They are surrounded by people filled with hatred, they dare not
look at one another directly, and in front of them they see a parade
of prisoners whose enslavement both contrasts with the limited
freedom which they have begun to achieve and suggests how their
relationship is likely to end.

In addition to its main action, the chapter contains some significant
details about the world of '1984'. There is **satire** on popular fiction
in the brief account of the Fiction Department. The presence of
telescreens monitoring the toilets is a reminder that privacy is now
almost non-existent. The manipulation of history is evident in
Victory Square, which is a renovated version of the present-day
Trafalgar Square, built to celebrate the British defeat of Napoleon's
fleet. It contains one of London's best-known landmarks, Nelson's
Column, commemorating the British commander who was killed in
the action, but the statue of Nelson has now been replaced by one
of Big Brother, and the square no longer commemorates the Battle
of Trafalgar but the Battle of Airstrip One, itself a 'rewriting' of the
Battle of Britain in the Second World War. The statue of the man
on horseback 'which was supposed to represent Oliver Cromwell'
(p. 120) is presumably the statue of King Charles I, Cromwell's
great enemy. How we respond to all these changes will depend to

some extent on our evaluation of the historical figures involved, but the cynical erasures of truth and reversals of meaning are clear.

Most critics accept that the love of Winston and Julia is a positive experience which contrasts firmly with the hatred stirred up by the Party, but that is not quite what this chapter tells us. The use of 'I' and 'you' in Julia's message presupposes a relationship between two people, but they have not met and as yet they know next to nothing about each other. How can somebody love a stranger? 'Love' here can only refer to sexual desire, which is certainly Winston's feeling, as the repeated references to Julia's 'youthful body' show. However, this is a very different feeling from the kind of love which Winston associates with his mother, that complete devotion to someone else which could lead you to sacrifice your life for them. Whether the relationship between Winston and Julia ever develops into this second type of love is a question which the reader of the book needs to bear in mind as the story develops.

CONTEXT

The Battle of Britain (July to October 1940), in which around 2,500 RAF pilots defeated the German air force and forestalled invasion, is generally regarded as one of the most heroic episodes of British history. Readers who had been saved from the Nazis by the Battle of Britain would have not looked kindly at its travestying as the Battle of Airstrip One.

CHAPTER 2

- Winston and the girl, Julia, meet up in the country as planned and make love.
- To Winston this is a political act because it places physical desire above Party discipline.

Winston and the girl, whose name is Julia, meet up as planned in the countryside. Winston realises that the place is very like his imagined ideal of the Golden Country. Julia proves to be a rebel against the Party, but of a very different kind to Winston. She has no thought of changing society and finds it easy to conform outwardly, but she greatly enjoys pleasure, particularly sexual fulfilment, and she has learned how to elude the Party's restrictions in order to achieve it. Winston is delighted to learn that she has had many lovers because it shows that the system is more corrupt than he had realised. They make love. To Winston this lovemaking is a political act because it asserts that physical desire is more important than obedience to the Party.

COMMENTARY

In this chapter Winston at last finds a relationship which offers fulfilment and which opens up a world of emotions and behaviour beyond those permitted by the Party. As usual, we are drawn into his feelings by **free indirect discourse**: for example the paragraph where he observes a thrush which becomes a **symbol** of his own natural feelings. His changing emotion and perceptions of the world are also signalled by an eruption of **metaphors** in the text. For most of the book **similes** are used for description, but the presence of Julia seems to so intensify Winston's feelings that mere comparisons are not strong enough and a more complete transformation is required. This begins in the previous chapter where he feels 'ice at his heart' (p. 118) and experiences a 'pale-coloured pleasure' (p. 120), but the first paragraph of this chapter has 'pools of gold', ground 'misty with bluebells', air which kisses the skin and a wood with a heart (p. 123). The contrast with Winston's experiences in every previous chapter makes this episode powerful, as does the resemblance of the landscape to the Golden Country of his dreams. The events are made more realistic by Winston's temporary impotence, which is a plausible reaction to Julia's sudden embrace, but careful readers may also have reservations about some aspects of their relationship.

When Winston asks Julia why she is attracted to him, the only answer he receives is that she can see from his face that he is a dissident. This is actually a worrying response because if she can easily read his expression, so might the Thought Police. It is also an unconvincing answer. Would she risk torture and death to have an affair with a man on such a slender basis, with no other attractions? Julia's unexplained desire for Winston and her access to real chocolate may revive our suspicion that she is trying to entrap him. If Julia is not a member of the Thought Police, her behaviour is actually quite hard to credit, arranging the meeting against all the difficulties, pulling Winston down on top of her, calling him 'darling' and so on. This seems more like a male fantasy than the likely behaviour of a young woman with an older man she has never met before. The impression is reinforced when, after knowing her for only a few minutes, Winston tells her that he recently wanted

CHECK THE BOOK

Beatrix Campbell argues in her essay 'Orwell – Paterfamilias or Big Brother?' (in Norris, 1984) that the portrayal of Julia as a sex object with no interest in ideas is typical of Orwell's negative attitude towards women, even when he is actually trying to be positive about them.

to rape and murder her, and her response is to laugh 'delightedly' (p. 127).

The likeliest explanation for these implausibilities is that Orwell is more interested in how Julia appears to Winston than he is in developing her as a character in her own right. In this she is like the proles and, aptly enough, she too is described with a slightly patronising animal simile, her swearing likened to 'the sneeze of a horse' (p. 129). When Julia conforms to Winston's dream of the Golden Country by tearing off her sash, she is in danger of being reduced to a wholly symbolic figure, reflecting Winston's view of life, not a rounded individual with whom he can develop a convincing relationship. This is not the only factor undermining the credibility and emotive power of their love. While Winston expects his affair with Julia to embody values which are the opposite of the Party's, he remains very much a Party man in construing sex as a political act and thinking of it as a diseased, corrupting force, associated with leprosy and syphilis. To fully oppose the Party's hatred would, logically, require selfless love, not 'undifferentiated desire' (p. 132).

CHAPTER 3

- Winston and Julia keep up their secret relationship.
- They learn more about one another.

Winston and Julia pursue their secret relationship, meeting as if by chance in a series of different locations and very occasionally making love in safe hiding places. Their relationship is a difficult one to maintain since it is hard to find times when they can both be free, and if there seems any chance of them being seen together by the authorities, they have to abandon their plans. On one occasion a rocket bomb falls quite close to them.

After the second time they make love, which they do in the belfry of a ruined church, they have more chance than usual to talk.

GLOSSARY

134 **bloody** irksome, annoying

134 **an atomic bomb** at the time the book was written, there was little appreciation of the long-term effects of nuclear radiation

CONTEXT

The USA had ended the war against Japan in 1945 by dropping atomic bombs on Hiroshima and Nagasaki, killing over 200,000 people.

Winston learns that Julia is twenty-six years old, works in Pornosec (the section of the Fiction Department which produces pornography for young proles) and has been having such love affairs for a decade. He wonders how many young people share her view, that any attempt to overthrow the Party is so futile as to be almost inconceivable but that it is nonetheless possible and even fun to have a good time secretly. Julia suggests to Winston that the Party represses sex because it needs its members to be frustrated and overheated, so that it can harness the resulting energy and aggression. Winston tells her how he once almost pushed his conformist wife over a cliff to be rid of her, and is now rather sorry he did not. Although Julia recognises that they will be caught by the Thought Police one day, she rejects Winston's preoccupation with this eventuality as morbid and urges him to enjoy what they are doing now.

COMMENTARY

This chapter develops the relationship between the two characters and in particular tells us more about Julia. We start *in media res*, continuing the episode of their first liaison, then move through summaries of their romance over the next month, focusing in particular on one meeting as an example of the general pattern. Although we do learn a lot more about Julia, it is arguable that she stays a rather two-dimensional figure, more effective as a **foil** to Winston than as a character in her own right. Even the description of her breasts as 'ripe yet firm' (p. 142) is something of a cliché – the kind of lifeless **metaphor** which Orwell condemns in his celebrated essay 'Politics and the English Language' (1946). She remains at the same level of **characterisation** as the proles in being practical but having little interest in ideas, and in this connection she is again compared to an animal, this time a rabbit. Despite her gender, she shares Winston's misogyny, remarking firmly, 'How I hate women!' (p. 136). When we are informed that she seemed to know 'the essential parts' of Winston's life already (p. 138), is this supposed to emphasise how typical of the Party his experience is, or is it a clue that she is working for the Thought Police and knows the information in advance? Winston's remark, 'We are the dead' (p. 142) is another **motif** introduced to give the book shape, and will be repeated later.

CHECK THE BOOK

'Politics and the English Language' is available in *Essays* (1994) and other collections of Orwell's writings.

CHAPTER 4

- Winston rents a room above the junk shop, so he and Julia can spend more time together.
- He is upset to find that rats can get into the room, as he has a great horror of them.

Winston rents a room above the junk shop and, with the connivance of the owner, Mr Charrington, he and Julia use it as a place where they can be together, almost as an ordinary couple would have lived back in the 'abolished past'. Winston knows that this is a dangerous expedient, since it makes discovery more likely, but as working hours have been increased with the approach of Hate Week, it has become more and more difficult for them to arrange meetings in any other way. When Julia first joins him in the room, she brings a bag full of luxuries which she has managed to obtain, items such as proper sugar, bread, coffee and tea, normally only available to members of the Inner Party. She tells Winston she has a surprise for him and makes him turn his back for a short while. During this time he listens to a large female prole singing a sentimental song while pegging out washing beneath their window, a figure he finds appealing in her closeness to natural life and her indifference to the concerns of the Party. When he looks round, the surprise turns out to be that Julia has bought some make-up and scent from a proletarian shop in order to make herself appear more feminine.

Winston is disturbed to find that rats are able to get into their room. He has a particular horror of them, associated with a recurring nightmare in which something terrible awaits him on the other side of 'a wall of darkness' (p. 151). He becomes even more upset when Julia starts telling him about how in some parts of London rats attack children. Later his mind turns again to the nursery rhyme 'Oranges and lemons', which Julia also knows, and to his glass paperweight, which seems to him to be a symbol of happiness and security.

GLOSSARY

145 **It's started early** 'It' refers to Julia's menstrual period

CONTEXT

Orwell had an especial fear of rats.

COMMENTARY

By hiring a room of their own, Winston and Julia are able to create a reality for themselves outside the world of Big Brother. Its fittings recall the early twentieth century, enabling them to approximate the way of life of the last period in history before the state, aided by technology, reached so deeply into individuals' lives that it dominated them. Even the clock has a 'twelve-hour face' (p. 143), contrasting with the twenty-four-hour clock which opens the book. The architectural **simile**, 'solid as a Norman pillar' (p. 144), links the regressive decor of the room and the timeless qualities of the anonymous prole woman singing outside. She has a key part to play in the book, as, for Winston, she and her kind embody the human feelings and way of life which people like him have lost. However, she is very much a passive figure, carrying out dull chores and singing a song which expresses loss and lack of fulfilment. The song has not even been made up by her or by a fellow prole, but is a set of clichés assembled by a machine.

Winston values the family life which the proles still have but to which he and Julia can only aspire. In a neat reversal of romantic convention, he wishes that they were a couple who had been comfortably married for ten years, not lovers who feel an urgent desire for each other. Winston's feelings are summed up in the important symbol of the paperweight. It has a simplicity and transparency which his own life lacks, his working time being devoted to constructing lies and his private life to a secret affair, and it also has a sense of depth rare in this era because it is an object which has survived unchanged for many years, not one manufactured for short-term use. Unfortunately, it is also fragile, and when Winston imagines it as the room with them inside it, our sense of their vulnerability is reinforced.

Readers who suspect Julia of being a Thought Police agent will again be suspicious of her ability to procure luxury goods, in this case coffee and other groceries. Even if we assume that she has obtained these goods through another lover, which might account for her reluctance to explain their origin, the scene in which they share them still carries a strong sense of doom rather than joy,

CHECK THE BOOK

Beatrix Campbell argues in her essay 'Orwell – Paterfamilias or Big Brother?' (in Norris, 1984) that the prole woman, despite Winston's efforts to invest her with positive associations, is a passive, pitiful figure, and that this reflects Orwell's limited understanding of working people, especially women.

as Winston reflects several times that they are bound to be caught within a few weeks. Later in the chapter his reaction to the presence of rats introduces a further ominous note, especially because, like so much else in the story, it is associated with one of his dreams, a nightmare of 'a wall of darkness' (p. 151) behind which waits something so awful that he cannot acknowledge it. Like the paperweight and the 'Oranges and lemons' nursery rhyme, which is again quoted in this chapter with its sinister ending 'here comes a chopper to chop off your head!' (p. 153), the rats are a motif to which the story will inevitably return.

CHAPTER 5

GLOSSARY
158 **pinchbeck** made of cheap material

- As Hate Week approaches, Winston and Julia find their secret room a welcome refuge from the ever more hysterical atmosphere that is being whipped up.

As Winston had predicted, Syme vanishes one day and all records of his existence are erased. The atmosphere of hysteria intensifies as preparations for Hate Week advance. Pamphlets, posters and a 'Hate Song' are used to stir emotion, so that even the proles are caught up, while rocket bombs fall on a cinema and a children's play area, leading to funeral processions and angry demonstrations. Winston and Julia find their secret room a valuable refuge from all this turmoil and Mr Charrington is happy to show them artefacts of the past and recite old nursery rhymes for them. Although Winston still fears they will be caught, for the moment he experiences renewed health and confidence. He and Julia continue to discuss the Party and their opposition to it. She assumes that secret dissent is common and she also suggests that the rocket bombs falling on London are sent by the Party to increase hatred of the enemy, but she has no real interest in the way that history has been falsified (she does not even recall the switch of enemy from Eastasia to Eurasia four years previously) and she does not understand why Winston considers the photograph of the three 'traitors' to be so important.

CONTEXT

German V1 and V2 missiles hit London during 1944, killing around 5,500 people before the launch sites were overrun by advancing Allied troops.

COMMENTARY

There are few new events in this chapter, but the atmosphere of oppression increases as Hate Week approaches, and the sense of danger is reinforced by the disappearance of Syme and by Julia's plausible suggestion that the rocket bombs falling on London are sent by the Party in order to stoke up popular anger. Parsons is an enthusiastic figure in the preparations for Hate Week, contrasting with Winston, who has become less excitable and more physically healthy than before due to his relationship with Julia. Mention of Parsons prepares us for his reappearance in a few chapters' time.

There is again a contrast between Winston and Julia. He is an intellectual with a sense of the past and a belief that it is necessary to examine the truth in order to live a worthwhile life; she accepts the Party's rule and rebels only at the level of her own personal freedom, having no belief that it could be possible or even worthwhile to overthrow the system. The information that we learn about Charrington, that he never seems to leave the building and never seems to have customers, further arouses our suspicions about him.

CONTEXT

Although Orwell invented the word 'unperson', the phenomenon was familiar from Stalin's Russia. When someone was 'purged', for example, photographs would be doctored so that the victim no longer appeared on a public platform with Stalin.

CHAPTER 6

- O'Brien invites Winston to visit him, in a way which causes Winston to believe it is an invitation to enter a conspiracy against the Party.

O'Brien asks Winston whether he knows that two of the words used in his articles have been made obsolete in the latest edition of the Newspeak Dictionary and invites him to his home to see a copy. In raising this subject, O'Brien mentions a friend of Winston's who is an expert on Newspeak. The reference can only be to Syme, but Syme is now an 'unperson' and any mention of him is a 'thoughtcrime'. This convinces Winston that O'Brien must be a conspirator against the Party who is covertly inviting him to make contact. Winston is anxious to do so, but is also frightened, because he believes it to be a further step towards his death.

COMMENTARY

This short chapter is an important one in the development of the story. Although Julia has brought Winston fulfilment, she is not a 'soul mate' with whom he can fully share his ideas. Winston has long dreamed that O'Brien might be such a person and now his hopes seem to be realised. It is odd that it does not occur to him that O'Brien might actually have been talking to Syme as his interrogator. Even so, Winston is still fearful of the consequences of becoming involved in a conspiracy against the Party and a **metaphor** is used to show the strength of his feeling, 'the sensation of stepping into the dampness of a grave' (pp. 166–7).

CHAPTER 7

- Winston dreams about his mother and sister.
- On waking, he talks to Julia about the importance of personal loyalty and the couple decide that, whatever happens to them, they will not betray one another.

Lying in bed with Julia, Winston dreams that he is inside the glass paperweight with his life spread out in front of him. He remembers that at an age between ten and twelve, after his father had disappeared, he would argue with his mother about how much of their meagre food supply he could have. One day he snatched his sister's chocolate ration and ran off. When he returned, his mother and sister had vanished, never to be seen again. Looking back, Winston admires his mother because she was motivated by authentic feelings, not rules imposed from outside, and she did what she felt was natural, instead of judging an act by what effect it might have in the longer term. Winston reflects that the proles still think this way, valuing acts in terms of their private loyalties, not by their contribution to history. He declares to Julia, who is now awake, that the proles are still human, but Party members like themselves are not. Their only hope is that, when they are finally taken to the Ministry of Love and are tortured, they do not betray one another.

COMMENTARY

The focus of the book again shifts from the external world to a dream of Winston's. This one seems to be a kind of therapeutic reliving of a suppressed memory, released by the natural existence which he has found with Julia which is **symbolised** by the paperweight. Although Winston himself does not explain it in such terms, it is a dream of guilt and it may show us the origins of some of his behaviour patterns, even his later willingness to be 'cured'. He has behaved badly towards his mother and his sister, perhaps the start of his lifelong misogyny, and he has acted as a selfish individual who breaks away from others, perhaps his first rebellion against society. To Winston 'the real point of the story' (p. 171) is that his mother's motivation was a more honourable one, based on love, than it seems possible for any Party member to possess now. In contrast to his earlier puzzled contempt for the proles, he now feels a respect for them because, even at the price of ignorance and defeat, they have retained the same view of life as his mother.

Winston and Julia discuss whether their own relationship can approximate this ideal of love. Interestingly, Julia, who was previously falling asleep, wakes up at this point and contributes the suggestion that they should not betray one another in their minds, whatever they are forced to say aloud. Those who think that Julia is working for the Thought Police could interpret this as a readying of Winston for the experience of Room 101, ensuring that when it comes his morale will be more easily shattered. The final sentence of the chapter sets out the horror at the core of the book, that there is no part of the self which can be preserved from invasion. Winston hopes that 'the inner heart, whose workings were mysterious even to yourself, remained impregnable' (p. 174), but this formulation carries the implication that an enemy sufficiently intelligent to understand your inner life, or to at least convince you that s/he understood it, could 'impregnate' you, turning you into a passive recipient, psychologically violated.

CHECK THE BOOK

George Woodcock in Part 4 of *The Crystal Spirit: A Study of George Orwell* (1967) observes that the emphasis on 'dreams and nightmares ... suggests that Orwell was very much aware of the importance of extra-rational elements in human life and – equally – in literary creation'.

CONTEXT

Orwell saw the British Fascist leader, Sir Oswald Mosley, address a public meeting in 1936 and was horrified by the way his black-shirted followers were allowed to attack hecklers.

CHAPTER 8

- Winston and Julia visit O'Brien.
- There they are inducted into the Brotherhood, a secret resistance organisation.

GLOSSARY

178 **dim memories of … a hoarding** Winston remembers a well-known neon advertisement for tonic wine in Piccadilly Circus

182 **persiflage** frivolous talk, banter

Winston and Julia go by separate routes to O'Brien's luxurious flat. They are amazed to discover that as a member of the Inner Party he is able to turn off his telescreen. Winston announces that he and Julia are thought-criminals, adulterers and enemies of the Party. The three of them, plus O'Brien's servant Martin, drink a toast of red wine to Goldstein, the leader of the Brotherhood. The couple swear that, for the cause of freedom, they are prepared to carry out a catalogue of crimes including murder, suicide and acts of sabotage which result in the deaths of innocent people, but they refuse to separate and never see one another again. O'Brien informs them that they will be sent a book describing the true nature of modern society and the strategy for its overthrow. The three drink a toast to the past. Julia leaves first so as to avoid suspicion. O'Brien tells Winston that he will receive 'the book' through an exchange of briefcases (p. 184). He suggests that they may meet again, but hesitates to say where. Remembering the dream mentioned in Part One, Chapter 2, Winston suggests, 'In the place where there is no darkness', and O'Brien seems to accept the phrase (p. 185). Winston asks him if he knows the 'Oranges and lemons' nursery rhyme, which he does.

COMMENTARY

The plural pronoun which opens this chapter – 'They had done it', rather than 'He had done it' – emphasises that Winston and Julia have become a couple (p. 174). Julia insists that they will never willingly part, even for the Brotherhood, a pledge to which Winston does not commit himself quite so forcefully. The meeting is chiefly one between Winston and O'Brien, and Julia is sent away early, leaving the two men together for an intimate exchange of ideas.

O'Brien seems the superior of Winston and Julia, not only because there is such a strong contrast between his well-appointed flat and the squalor which is normal in '1984', but also because he possesses a power and freedom greater than theirs. He is able to turn off the telescreen, he has a mysterious servant, he speaks of becoming a different person with a different face and, most of all, he knows about the Brotherhood and its operations. Winston regards him with a feeling 'almost of worship' (p. 182), putting a faith in him which will cause him problems in the final part of the book. Even so, it is surprising that he so readily accepts O'Brien's access to his own inner world. Not only does O'Brien seem to recognise the phrase 'In the place where there is no darkness', which Winston dreamed he said to him in Part One, Chapter 2, but O'Brien actually repeats Winston's own phrase 'We are the dead' (p. 183) from Part Two, Chapter 3, a phrase which he could not have heard unless he was spying on him in some way. Perhaps we should remember that, despite its **naturalistic** features, this is not a **realistic** novel, but a fantastic tale of an individual trapped between the external world and his own dreams and nightmares, which increasingly resemble and reinforce one another.

The same problem of how realistically we should read the book, but in a form somewhat harder to ignore, is posed by the pledge which Winston and Julia make to carry out various terrible acts, including throwing sulphuric acid in a child's face. At one level, Orwell is making an irrefutable point, that anyone who embarks on a war is bound to cause suffering to the innocent and must accept some degree of guilt. *Nineteen Eighty-Four* was written soon after the Second World War and perhaps Orwell wished to question the depiction of warfare as heroic which was naturally prevalent at that time. At another level, the couple's unthinking acquiescence in terrorism must make us dubious about the seriousness of their commitment to build a better society. Although we are told later that O'Brien's tone makes the horrific acts seem acceptable, there is no escaping the fact that Winston and Julia have not really thought through the implications of their rebellion. We may even feel that we as readers have not sufficiently considered these issues either. Conversely, the final implication of the couple's vows may be that, in a world where the government allows no opposition and defines for its citizens what is good and bad, it is almost impossible for someone who rebels against the Party to do so without becoming corrupt, and the fault here lies more in the Party than in the rebels.

CONTEXT

Is Winston agreeing to be a freedom fighter or a terrorist? The attack on the World Trade Center in New York in 2001, resulting in the deaths of over 3,000 people, may help modern readers appreciate the full significance of Winston's 'Yes' to O'Brien's questions.

CHAPTER 9

- Oceania is suddenly at war with Eastasia instead of Eurasia.
- Workers at the Ministry of Truth have to work overtime in order to revise all the materials which indicate the contrary.
- Once this is done, Winston returns to the room above the junk shop, meets up with Julia and begins to read the Brotherhood's secret book which has now been passed to him.

On the sixth day of Hate Week, Winston is taking part in a demonstration in a square in central London when news arrives that Oceania is no longer at war with Eurasia but with Eastasia. In turn Eurasia has become an ally. There is no explicit acknowledgement, however, that there has been any change in policy. Instead, the banners and posters bearing the wrong pictures and slogans are explained as the work of saboteurs. In two or three minutes they have been torn down and everyone is behaving as though Oceania has always been at war with Eastasia. In the confusion someone slips Winston a briefcase containing '*the book*' (p. 187).

Everyone at the Ministry of Truth now has to work overtime in order to revise all the published materials which mention war with Eurasia or alliance with Eastasia, although no one ever admits openly that this is what they are doing. After a week of intense activity, the task is completed and the workers are given an afternoon off. Winston retreats to the room above the junk shop and begins reading the book which he has been sent by the Brotherhood, *The Theory and Practice of Oligarchical Collectivism* by Emmanuel Goldstein. Julia joins him and he reads her some of the text aloud.

The book explains that the three superstates are so evenly matched that the war between them can never be won. The main purpose of the conflict is not to secure victory, but to create a siege mentality and with it the material conditions which enable a small caste of people to remain in total control. The external threat is used to justify the centralisation of power, and the scarcity of goods

CONTEXT

James Burnham's book *The Managerial Revolution* (1941) suggested that a new class of managers would take power in three superstates centred on Europe, Asia and America, which would then engage in perpetual warfare. Orwell drew on Burnham's ideas in *Nineteen Eighty-Four*, though he had strong reservations about Burnham's underestimation of the power of democracy.

CHECK THE BOOK

Orwell's essay 'The Prevention of Literature' can be found in *Essays* (1994) and other collections of his writings.

increases the importance which possessions have as markers of privilege, making society more steeply hierarchical. In all three states, the rulers have been able to take advantage of the war to achieve absolute control of their populations, cutting them off from the past and from other cultures, so that the only knowledge they have is the knowledge which their rulers choose to give them. In the past it has been normal for a ruling class to be overthrown by a revolution. Once new rulers are in power, they become the next ruling class and are overthrown in their turn. The members of the Inner Party have been able to stop this process by using modern technology to manipulate and monitor the population, and by perverting the ideals of socialism. Socialists had believed that if wealth and power were taken from capitalists and put under state control, the result would be a free and equal society in which there was no ruling class and therefore no more need for conflict. While the Party did take the wealth and power from the capitalists, it then retained it for its own members, leaving the rest of the population with even less freedom than before. All the distinctive features of modern society, including doublethink and the falsification of history, exist in order to preserve this situation. Winston falls asleep before he can read the next section of the book, which promises to explain the Party's motives.

COMMENTARY

The sudden change of enemy from Eurasia to Eastasia during a political rally is one of the most striking episodes in the book. Some critics have objected that it is unbelievable, but the scene is clearly meant to be a ridiculous one, **satirising** diplomatic inconsistency. Orwell observes in his essay 'The Prevention of Literature' (1946) that throughout the 1930s a British Communist or 'fellow-traveller' was required to hate Nazi Germany, but once the Nazi–Soviet pact of September 1939 made Russia and Germany allies, he or she was expected to sympathise with the Hitler regime. Twenty months later, when the Germans invaded Russia, the situation was at once reversed. 'Immediately after hearing the 8 o'clock news bulletin on the morning of 22 June 1941, he had to start believing once again that Nazism was the most hideous evil the world had ever seen.' Orwell specifies the exact time at which the change took place in order to make it seem more absurd, and in the Hate Week episode he takes the same device to a dramatic extreme. Orwell's target is not simply Communists, however, for the 1941 invasion made all British citizens allies of the Soviet Union. After it, Stalin and his regime were portrayed favourably in Allied propaganda. It was for this reason that Orwell found it impossible to get his anti-Soviet satire *Animal Farm* published until 1945, by which time the Russians had replaced the Germans as Britain's chief enemy and he found himself the author of a surprise bestseller.

The frantic rewriting of history which follows Oceania's change of ally prevents Winston reading '*the book*' for several days, a delay which naturally increases our curiosity about its contents. *The Theory and Practice of Oligarchical Collectivism* has also attracted objections from some critics. The insertion of several pages of discussion into the narrative is, after all, quite a crude way to expand upon the book's themes and it certainly holds up the story. If we were to read *Nineteen Eighty-Four* as a conventional novel which develops relationships between believable characters, then Goldstein's arguments would seem intrusive, even more so than the essay on 'The Principles of Newspeak', which is at least confined to an appendix. However, judged as a conventional novel, *Nineteen Eighty-Four* is a clumsy piece of work altogether and it is more appropriate to see it as quite a different type of book (see **Literary background**). It is a **science fiction dystopia** and we read such a book not for subtle **characterisation** but for its author's imaginative treatment of society. We expect, and accept, long passages of exposition provided that these are integrated sufficiently into the narrative. It is a matter of individual judgement whether, in this context, Goldstein's writings are sufficiently integrated. Some critics have felt that the extracts are too long and that they diminish our interest in the characters at a crucial moment in the book. Others have judged, on the contrary, that the story has carefully developed our curiosity about the society of '1984' so that we are now eager to read Goldstein's views. The extracts clarify the situation and issues at a timely moment, leaving us free thereafter to concentrate on Winston's fate. Orwell himself strongly defended the Goldstein sections and refused to cut them for a book club edition, stating in a letter of 1949, 'A book is built up as a balanced structure and one cannot simply remove large chunks here and there unless one is ready to recast the whole thing'.

 CHECK THE BOOK
The frustrations that Orwell experienced in trying to publish *Animal Farm* are vividly described in Chapter 15 of *Orwell: The Life* by D. J. Taylor (2003).

 CHECK THE BOOK
Goldstein's views are based on the well-known account of class society in the *Communist Manifesto* by Karl Marx and Friedrich Engels (1848).

CHAPTER 10

- The Thought Police take Winston and Julia prisoner.

When Winston and Julia wake it has begun to grow dark. Thinking of the mass of people all around the world who are not members of the political elite and who care only for the fundamentals of life, Winston repeats his phrase describing Party members, 'We are the dead' (p. 230), and is aghast to hear it repeated by a voice from behind the picture on the wall. The voice orders them to stand back to back with their hands clasped behind their heads, then recites the ending of the nursery rhyme 'Oranges and lemons': 'here comes a chopper to chop off your head!' (p. 231). Uniformed men break into the room through the window. The paperweight is smashed and Julia punched in the stomach. Mr Charrington enters the room but, having discarded much of his former disguise, he is now revealed as an officer of the Thought Police, the one who spoke to them from the hidden telescreen.

QUESTION

How far do you think we should empathise with Winston and how far should we disagree with his reactions and views?

COMMENTARY

Winston awakens with a feeling of conviction about what really matters in life, which he sees as exemplified in the prole woman in the yard, though he still thinks of her in animal terms, as a creature with 'mare-like' buttocks (p. 228). The whole of nature, including most of the human race in all countries, lives free of the Party's mental confinement. One day the Party must fall and be succeeded by 'a race of conscious beings' (p. 230) combining the natural life of the proles with the intellectual awareness of the educated. Appropriately, it is at this moment, when Winston has at last developed a view of life distinct from the Party's, that the Thought Police take him prisoner and take up the challenge of destroying it.

One aspect of the arrest stressed in the story but generally passed over in silence by commentators, presumably because they do not know what to make of it, is Winston's conviction that the time of day does not correspond to the time on the clock and, linked to this, Julia's puzzlement that the oil in the stove has run out. We are never given an explanation for these anomalies. Could it be that the lovers have been drugged and the Thought Police have been busy in the room, for example installing the telescreen behind the picture? The effect is a disturbing and sinister one. Like Winston, we cannot understand what is happening or predict what may ensue. We can only await further developments with alarm.

The capture of Winston and Julia is dismaying, so much so that as we read it, caught up in the story, we overlook its implausibility. It would be far more sensible for the Thought Police to have entered the room while the couple were asleep. If the arresting squad was not ready in time, they could still creep quietly into the room and ambush the lovers, reducing their opportunity to produce weapons and defend themselves. The course the Thought Police actually adopt – announcing their impending arrival through the telescreen, then storming the room by the stairs and window – is ridiculous. The reason Orwell arranges events in this way is to make them more dramatic, and in this he is almost entirely successful. It is true that the voice which says 'You are the dead' is a rather 'stagey' device, but even this has quite a powerful effect in restoring the sense of being watched and controlled which Winston had begun to feel he had lost. The violent intrusions into the room, the beating of Julia and the entry of the transformed Charrington rapidly turn the safe haven into a place of horror. The **realism** of Winston's desire to urinate adds to the effect. The breaking of the paperweight **symbolises** the destruction of privacy and truth, as is indicated by Winston's response, where the adverbial 'always' invites the reader to see the wider significance of this act of destruction (p. 232).

(See **Text 2** of **Extended commentaries** for a more detailed discussion of part of this chapter.)

CONTEXT

Czeslaw Milosz, a Pole living under totalitarianism in 1952, confirmed Orwell's insight into the Soviet system. He had managed to obtain a copy of Orwell's book, even though it was banned like Goldstein's. 'Even those who know Orwell only by hearsay are amazed that a writer who never lived in Russia should have so keen a perception into its life.'

PART THREE

CHAPTER 1

- Winston meets several other people who have been arrested, including his conformist colleague Parsons and two people who are terrified of being sent to Room 101.
- Eventually he discovers that one of his captors is O'Brien.

After being held temporarily in a crowded cell where political prisoners are mixed with ordinary criminals, Winston is locked on his own in a cell containing a lavatory pan, a bench and four telescreens. He is forbidden to make any movement. Two or three hours later, the poet Ampleforth (glimpsed briefly in Part One, Chapter 4, and Part Two, Chapter 1) is put in with him. Ampleforth cannot think what he has done wrong, except to retain the word 'God' in a poem for lack of another word to rhyme with 'rod' (p. 242).

After he has gone, Parsons, the man Winston had predicted would never be vaporised, is put into the cell. His daughter has denounced him for saying, 'Down with Big Brother' in his sleep (p. 245). Parsons is proud of her, however, and accepts his punishment. When Parsons has to use the toilet Winston tries to cover his eyes but is ordered from the telescreen not to do so. Eventually Parsons is taken away and a number of other prisoners come and go, including a woman who seems particularly terrified when ordered to Room 101.

Finally there are six people in the cell. One is clearly dying of starvation and another, taking pity on him, tries to offer him a piece of bread. For this he is badly beaten by the guards. The starving man is then ordered to Room 101. Before he is taken out, he screams that he would rather face any other punishment than Room 101, including watching his own family's throats being cut, and tries to persuade the guards that the man who attempted to help him is the one that they should take. When Winston has again been alone for several hours, O'Brien enters, not as a prisoner, but as one of the

CHECK THE BOOK

Orwell's essay 'Rudyard Kipling' is in *Essays* (1994) and other collections of his writings.

officials in charge. With him is a guard who strikes Winston's elbow with a truncheon, then laughs as he writhes on the ground.

COMMENTARY

In Part One we saw and shared Winston's revulsion at the world of '1984'. In Part Two we followed his struggle to build an alternative world and view of life. Now his private world has been destroyed. In Part Three his view of life, too, is systematically broken down. The first stage of the process, recounted in Chapter 1, is to demoralise Winston so that he loses faith in his power to resist. He is placed in primitive, shared conditions which undermine his self-respect. He is treated in a way which classifies him as inferior even to ordinary criminals. His autonomy is removed by the telescreen's control of his every movement. Perhaps worst of all, he is kept in a state of constant fear. He does not know where he is or what exactly is going to happen to him, but repeatedly seeing the condition and treatment of other prisoners, none of whom seem able to stand up to their tormentors, makes him expect the very worst.

Among Winston's cellmates we are surprised to see not only Ampleforth, apparently brought in for a trivial error, but also Parsons, whom Winston had predicted would never be punished. The error is important. It reminds us at this crucial moment that Winston is not an entirely reliable interpreter of events and that, to arrive at the truth, we may have to disagree with his conclusions. The presence of both men also demonstrates the fanaticism of the authorities who will not overlook, it is plain, even the slightest deviance.

The unsparing description of Bumstead's beating is one of the most shocking moments in the book. In contrast, the man whom he had tried to help makes a melodramatic contribution to the chapter with his outburst, 'I've got a wife and three children. The biggest of them isn't six years old. You can take the whole lot of them and cut their throats in front of my eyes, and I'll stand by and watch it. But not Room 101!' (p. 249). It is hard to believe that any distressed person would express their feelings in so theatrical a fashion. There are several references to Room 101 in this chapter which do succeed in building suspense, but this clumsy attempt to foreshadow the

 QUESTION

When did you realise that O'Brien was a member of the Thought Police and why?

CONTEXT

Orwell had known a J. Bumstead, the son of a grocer in Southwold, where his parents lived. The unusual name must have stuck in his memory.

betrayal to come is not one of them. In this connection, it is surprising to note that Winston already retains few feelings for Julia. 'He felt no love for her, and he hardly even wondered what was happening to her' (p. 240). If their love is so easily overshadowed, then its extirpation does not seem to present much of a challenge to the Party.

Perhaps fearing that Winston's constant suffering might make the book monotonous, Orwell introduces some **comic relief** into this chapter, not only through the incorrigible conformity of Parsons, but through the behaviour of a **stereotypical** prostitute whom Winston speculates might be his mother. Even Winston's failure to realise why O'Brien has come into the cell strikes a darkly humorous note.

CHAPTER 2

• O'Brien tries to convert Winston to the view that whatever the Party states to be true must be so, using torture and drugs to reinforce his argument.

Winston is beaten viciously and repeatedly, then interrogated until he signs a series of preposterous confessions. After suffering hallucinations, he awakens strapped to a bed with O'Brien standing over him. O'Brien first demonstrates that he is able to cause Winston terrible pain by simply turning a dial, then tells him that he is 'mentally deranged' and must be cured (p. 258). He explains to Winston that the belief that there is a reality independent of the Party's account of it is false. If the Party can control all records and memories, then logically it must be able to define what is real and what is not. The war with Eurasia and the news report about the three 'traitors' must by definition be hallucinations. Winston had written in his diary that 'Freedom is the freedom to say that two plus two equals four'. Now O'Brien holds up four fingers and, by repeatedly inflicting pain, almost brings Winston to believe that he can see five.

After Winston has been given an injection of a drug which makes him feel positive about his captor, O'Brien goes on to explain that the Party's aim is not to secure a confession or to punish him, but to convert him so that he accepts their version of reality before he is executed. Pads are put on Winston's temples and an electrical charge put through him, then various beliefs of the Party are recited to him and he finds himself starting to believe them, including the proposition that O'Brien is holding up five fingers. At the end of the session, Winston is allowed to ask questions. O'Brien returns few clear answers to them, except to state that Julia betrayed Winston immediately she was interrogated and underwent a 'textbook' conversion (p. 271).

COMMENTARY

In this chapter Winston is further degraded and brutalised, so that the identity he has built up can be wiped away and replaced by a Party substitute. In the opening paragraph he is strapped to a bed, ready to be operated on by people with the latest technology for inflicting pain. Winston has already been reduced to the role of victim by a series of beatings and humiliations which are summarised over the next few pages. These events are mixed up with actual nightmares, for Winston's inner and outer lives again converge as they did when his mind was struggling to free itself from the tyranny of official beliefs. Ominously, a dream of 'laughter' and being 'forgiven' suggests that at least part of Winston wants to be accepted and reintegrated into the 'normal' world, preferably without having to face the 'dreadful thing' (p. 255) which may await him in Room 101.

The constant but unseen presence of O'Brien suggests that the latter is somehow part of Winston's own mind or even an all-seeing being like God, an impression reinforced when O'Brien comes into view and is able to look into Winston's mind and tell him exactly what he is thinking. O'Brien resembles 'a doctor, a teacher, even a priest' (p. 257), rather than a torturer. Fatally for his ability to resist, Winston does not regard O'Brien as an enemy out to destroy his existence. Instead, partly as a result of the extreme pressure to which he has been subjected, partly through natural human feelings

CHECK THE BOOK
George Woodcock argues in Part 4 of *The Crystal Spirit: A Study of George Orwell* (1967) that the political and human aspects of the book ought to come together powerfully in this episode, but instead the human betrayal tends to be overshadowed by O'Brien's long speeches about power.

of guilt and inadequacy, he is willing to consider that O'Brien is a 'protector', ready to teach him a new and more appropriate view of life. After all, his opponent is the only person he knows who shares his concerns and understands what happens in his soul. 'Perhaps one did not want to be loved so much as to be understood' (p. 264). As Winston passes from torture to tutorial, he is offered a firm, orthodox view of life to replace the sanely provisional one which he had begun to develop as a thinking individual.

O'Brien specifically distinguishes this view and the methods by which it is imposed, from those of the German Nazis and Russian Communists, and places all three in the tradition of the Christian Church of the Middle Ages. Contrary to the assumption of some readers, therefore, Orwell's book is not simply an attack on Soviet Communism. Perceiving that Fascism and Communism are not ordinary political movements but secularised religions, Orwell tries to show us the essence of the fanatical desire to transform the world which is a recurrent danger and can take many forms. The chapter contains numerous words and phrases with religious associations: 'confession', 'priest', 'martyrdoms', 'Inquisition', 'heretic', 'Thou shalt not' and 'penitence'. The idea that O'Brien can hold up three, four and five fingers simultaneously may be intended to **parody** the Christian doctrine of the trinity. The idea that Big Brother is immortal certainly equates him with God. (See **Critical Approaches: Satire** for further religious parallels.) The philosophical argument which rationalises this deification of Big Brother is put clearly by O'Brien. Reality is not 'objective, external, existing in its own right' (p. 261) but 'exists in the human mind', and it exists not on the basis of individual experience, but as a collective tradition handed on by those in authority.

In the midst of all this philosophical discussion, Orwell is careful to retain the forward movement of the story. We remain anxious to see whether Winston will give in to O'Brien, and at the end of the chapter further references to the mysterious Room 101 maintain suspense.

CONTEXT

In 1926, after Mussolini escaped the fourth attempt on his life, the Pope declared that his survival showed the Fascist dictator was being protected by God.

CHAPTER 3

- O'Brien explains that the Party desires total control of reality.

The process of 're-integration' continues, passing from 'learning' through 'understanding' towards 'acceptance' (p. 273). O'Brien explains that the Party seeks power for its own sake, as the ultimate good. They have discarded the pretence which even the Nazis and the Communists retained, that their ultimate aim is to set others free. They also realise that total power can only be achieved and retained collectively, not by individuals, and that total power is power over the mind. They can deny that the earth goes round the sun or that human beings evolved from earlier creatures, and so long as they control everyone's minds, these denials are effectively true. In the long term, the Party's goal is to create a world of fear, anger and self-abasement, with no families, no sexual pleasure, no art, no science, no love except love of Big Brother, no laughter except the laughter of triumph when an enemy is defeated. O'Brien tells Winston that the image which best sums up the future is 'a boot stamping on a human face – for ever' (p. 280). Winston tries to object that the Party's project is against human nature, but O'Brien talks down his objections, claiming that 'Men are infinitely malleable' (p. 282). He derides Winston's claim to represent a conception of humanity superior to the Party's, playing him a recording of his pledge (made in Part Two, Chapter 8) to commit dreadful crimes if the Brotherhood require it and showing him in a mirror how physically degraded he has become. The only humiliation Winston has not undergone, as he himself tells O'Brien, is that in his heart he has not yet betrayed Julia.

COMMENTARY

It is in this chapter that Winston and O'Brien set out their different viewpoints most explicitly. Insofar as the book is a discussion of ideas, this chapter is therefore its centrepiece. Orwell follows the example of Aldous Huxley's *Brave New World* in placing this key discussion near the conclusion, shortly before the central character is destroyed by the world he seeks to escape. Like Mond the World

Controller in Huxley's book, O'Brien asserts that there is no God and that therefore whatever the human species can be brought to believe is effectively the truth. O'Brien also resembles Mond in embracing the reconstruction of human nature by science, claiming that human beings can be manipulated into any form of behaviour, and endorsing the abolition of sexual reproduction and the family, leaving the individual totally dependent upon the state for upbringing and values. Unlike Mond, O'Brien does not claim that his regime is intended to set humanity free. On the contrary, he glories in the evil that it does.

In place of religion, O'Brien sets up the love of power, though paradoxically his language remains religious – 'We are the priests of power … God is power' (p. 276) – and his opposition to the findings of modern science and reinstatement of the belief that the earth is the centre of the universe look back to fundamentalist Christianity and the Inquisition. (In contrast, the barman in Part One, Chapter 8 uses the phrase 'we were all living in the treetops' (p. 91), suggesting that the proles, at least, still accept biological evolution.) Again, Orwell's target is not simply Communism or Fascism, but all systems of ideas, secular or spiritual, which claim to give an authoritative account of reality and are forcibly imposed upon people with no regard for individual experience. All such systems deny that significant meaning can be found in the relations between people and instead try to connect the individual to a greater scheme, imagined as a body in which people are mere cells. Recollecting that he has not betrayed Julia, Winston retains a last, desperate affiliation to the former belief.

(See **Text 3** of **Extended commentaries** for a more detailed description of part of this chapter.)

 CHECK THE BOOK

Chapter 3 of John Gribbin's *Science: A History* (2002) describes how the Catholic authorities threatened Galileo with torture to make him deny that the earth could be in orbit around the sun.

CONTEXT

In 1870 the Vatican General Council declared that the Pope was infallible when defining doctrine on faith and morals.

CHAPTER 4

- Winston tries hard to acquire the mentality which the Party demands, but cannot lose his old emotions. His love still belongs to Julia, not to Big Brother.
- When he cries out to her in a dream, O'Brien decides it is time to send him to Room 101.

Life improves for Winston. Although his accommodation, health care and food are not good, they are better than they were previously. He begins to recover something of his morale and his physical health. He feels that he has done what the Party requires of him. He now accepts that their view of things must prevail over his own. He even tries to train his mind to forget his previous objections, accepting that it is not enough to agree with the Party; he must prevent any thoughts of dissent occurring to him. One night he dreams happily of his execution, shot in the back of the head while walking down a corridor, but to his horror he awakes to the realisation that he has been shouting out his love for Julia. Now he has to admit that deep down he still hates the Party and hopes that, when he is shot, he will have preserved some of that hatred, so that they will not have succeeded in fully converting him before his death. O'Brien confronts him over his outburst, observing that he has largely been healed intellectually, but that he has failed to make progress emotionally. Winston confesses that although he is willing to obey Big Brother, he does not love him, he hates him. He is sent to Room 101.

CHECK THE BOOK
Margaret Atwood's novel *The Handmaid's Tale* (1985) and Arthur Miller's play *The Crucible* (1953) both depict societies which repress the individual, and can therefore be compared to *Nineteen Eighty-Four*.

COMMENTARY

This chapter is a kind of false conclusion, offering the reader a plausible and comparatively gentle end to Winston's rebellion. Winston has accepted the Party line, but the narrator depicts his acceptance in an **ironic** tone which ensures we still see the defeat for what it is. The opening sentence 'He was much better' (p. 287) is clearly Winston's opinion, presented to us through **free indirect discourse**. We are not intended to agree that he is 'better', but to see that word as a perversion of the truth. Similarly, we do not take the improved conditions of Winston's life at face value. His 'new set of dentures' (p. 287) would not be needed if his old teeth and gums had not been ruined by beatings and starvation. For Winston, however, there seems no way forward but to accept all things at the Party's evaluation and he patiently trains himself to accept its teachings, even the proposition that two plus two equals five, which in Part One, Chapter 7 he had seen as the epitome of oppression. Yet the beliefs Winston forces on himself never form a connection with the deeper world of his dreams. It is not surprising, therefore, that when he does dream, the feelings for Julia which he has had to repress burst back to the surface. As O'Brien realises, they can only be rooted out if Winston experiences emotions so powerful that they penetrate into the depths of his soul, and, at last, therefore, he is ordered to Room 101.

CONTEXT

Some people have claimed that Room 101 was the number of Orwell's office at the BBC, but this does not seem to have been the case.

CHAPTER 5

- In Room 101 Winston's face is attached to a wire cage full of rats, his worst fear.
- He screams for the pain to be applied to Julia instead of to him.

Room 101 is in the depths of the Ministry of Love. It is where individuals are exposed to their very worst fear. In Winston's case the fear is of rats. He is strapped into a chair and O'Brien starts to attach a cage full of rats to his face. Winston begs O'Brien to tell him what he wants him to say or do, but O'Brien will not help him. Eventually Winston screams out for the pain to be applied to Julia instead of to him, and the cage is not opened.

COMMENTARY

This short chapter is the climax of Winston's story. In some respects, it is a powerful piece of writing. We have shared Winston's point of view throughout the book and it is impossible for us now to respond with detachment. We feel that we are there with him, facing the ultimate horror as O'Brien gradually brings it into view. The language of the book has previously tended to become

metaphorical at moments of emotional intensity, and here Winston's experiences are so extreme that, to express his emotions of isolation and suffering, he first hallucinates a desert plain, then outer space. In these frenzied moments, we hardly question O'Brien's ability to see into Winston's mind and comment on his dream of 'a wall of blackness' (p. 297).

Several critics have found the threat of the rats a banal one to represent ultimate horror. This may be so, though one suspects that if these critics were personally exposed to the threat they might change their minds. More to the point, the episode is diminished because Winston's exclamation 'Do it to Julia!' (p. 300) is not brought about convincingly. We are told that Winston 'suddenly understood' this was his only chance of escape (p. 299). How does he work this out? And how does the belief relate to his relationship with her, already indicated to be problematic, and his sense of identity and self-respect? To make matters worse, his outburst is as stagey as that of the starving man in Part Three, Chapter 2: 'Tear her face off, strip her to the bones' (p. 300). These lurid injunctions suggest that, rather than betraying the love of his life, Winston is reverting to the sadistic fantasies he entertained about her when he thought she was a spy. His love for her has not been shown sufficiently forcefully earlier in the book for its destruction here to seem the total, heartbreaking reversal that is implied.

CHECK THE FILM

In Michael Radford's film *1984* (1984), Winston actually sees Julia standing beyond the cage of rats. It is unclear whether he is hallucinating or whether she is placed there to suggest to him that betrayal of her is his one chance to escape.

CHAPTER 6

- After his 'conversion', Winston becomes one of the former 'traitors' who sit at the Chestnut Tree Café awaiting eventual execution.

- He reflects on his past and future, thinks of his one meeting with Julia since they were released, and listens to news of a military victory.

- He no longer has any feelings of hostility to the system; he loves Big Brother.

GLOSSARY

302 **sinecure** a position requiring little or no work

308 **ghosts fading at cock-crow** echoes *Hamlet* I.1.147

310 **colossus that bestrode the world** echoes *Antony and Cleopatra* V.2.82–3

Winston's betrayal of Julia removes his final mental defence and he is fully converted. He is given a new job and, like the three 'traitors' he saw in the '1960s', spends much of his time at the Chestnut Tree Café. While listening to an announcement from the telescreen of a military victory, he thinks back to his sole meeting with Julia after they had been released. Neither of them felt love; each confessed to betrayal of the other. He also recalls happy scenes of his childhood, but pushes them out of his memory. As the telescreen confirms the important victory, Winston thinks ahead to his execution and can feel only love for Big Brother.

COMMENTARY

The opening three words of the chapter, 'The Chestnut Tree', tell us all we need to know (p. 300). Winston has been successfully 'brainwashed' and is now installed in the café where traitors await their execution. That he is sitting in his 'usual' corner indicates that he has been a patron of the café for some time and therefore his death cannot be far off. As in Part Two, Chapter 4, the narration remains focused on Winston, but is **ironic** in tone and content. We and the narrator share his thoughts ('Oceania had always been at war with Eurasia', p. 301), but we do not share his beliefs and opinions. When he traces '2 + 2 = 5' on the table, we can see that he has lost touch with the reality he once defended (p. 303).

When Winston recalls his final meeting with Julia, it means nothing to him. Nor, most poignantly of all, does his memory of playing snakes and ladders as a child. Introduced at this important stage of the story, the game is surely meant to have a **symbolic** meaning, the snakes perhaps representing temptation, as in the Book of Genesis in the Bible, and the ladders redemption. Winston, however, is unable to put past sins behind him. There is no one to forgive him. Julia is a fellow sinner, and an unforgiving Big Brother has replaced a potentially merciful God. Winston no longer plays snakes and ladders but chess, which deals in a straightforward battle between good and evil. In his defeated state Winston associates good or white with Big Brother, but we the readers know that evil has simply disguised itself, and that in the world in which Winston is trapped madness and sickness are posing as sanity and health.

> **CONTEXT**
>
> Most British editions of the book between 1951 and 1989 have '2 + 2 = ', a misprint which may erroneously suggest that Winston is not fully 'converted'.

It is impossible to tell whether the telescreen's claims of victory at the end of the book are substantial or not. Has Oceania really won a victory which may enable it to defeat Eurasia or is this merely another piece of 'spin'? Beaten into gullibility, Winston accepts what he hears at face value and is overcome with love for Big Brother. The tone of the last paragraph is uncertain, and different readers have interpreted it differently. One influential writer has even viewed it as **comical**, but this reading seems difficult to sustain. We might be closer to the truth thinking of it as a sad contempt. Winston's soul is already dead. He is a pathetic figure, almost beyond pity. The time has come to turn from him and make up our minds that we ourselves will avoid such a fate by opposing even the beginnings of totalitarianism.

APPENDIX: THE PRINCIPLES OF NEWSPEAK

The appendix elaborates the description of Newspeak given by Syme in Part One, Chapter 5. Orwell clearly thought that the concept of Newspeak was one which deserved development (rightly, since it is a thought-provoking idea which has generated much lively discussion over the years), but to insert an essay on Newspeak into the main part of the book, however disguised, would hold up the story and distract the reader. While it would be difficult to disagree with this conclusion, some readers have felt that even putting the ideas into an appendix is a clumsy device, making for an awkward reading experience. However, it is possible to argue that *Nineteen Eighty-Four* is not a conventional novel in which the interest lies in characters and their relationships, but a discursive work where such an appendix is acceptable. Margaret Atwood's *The Handmaid's Tale* (1985), a more recent book of a similar type which is sometimes studied in comparison to *Nineteen Eighty-Four*, also has an appendix written from a future perspective which provokes similar disagreements.

The fact that the appendix is written in the past tense, and in Oldspeak, raises one last question. Is the past tense simply a convenient device for Orwell to employ, or does the discussion of Newspeak as a piece of history imply that the appendix dates

CHECK THE BOOK

There are illuminating discussions of Newspeak and the linguistic thinking behind it in David Wykes's *A Preface to Orwell* (1987) and Roger Fowler's *The Language of George Orwell* (1995).

from a further point in the future, when the Party system has been overthrown? If so, the book ends on a more hopeful note than many readers have realised.

EXTENDED COMMENTARIES

TEXT 1 – PART ONE, CHAPTER 6 (PP. 70–2)

Winston sighed inaudibly. He picked up his pen again and wrote:

> *She threw herself down on the bed, and at once, without any kind of preliminary, in the most coarse, horrible way you can imagine, pulled up her skirt. I—*

He saw himself standing there in the dim lamplight, with the smell of bugs and cheap scent in his nostrils, and in his heart a feeling of defeat and resentment which even at that moment was mixed up with the thoughts of Katharine's white body, frozen for ever by the hypnotic power of the Party. Why did it always have to be like this? Why could he not have a woman of his own instead of these filthy scuffles at intervals of years? But a real love affair was an almost unthinkable event. The women of the Party were all alike. Chastity was as deeply ingrained in them as Party loyalty. By careful early conditioning, by games and cold water, by the rubbish that was dinned into them at school and in the Spies and the Youth League, by lectures, parades, songs, slogans and martial music, the natural feeling had been driven out of them. His reason told him that there must be exceptions, but his heart did not believe it. They were all impregnable, as the Party intended that they should be. And what he wanted, more even than to be loved, was to break down that wall of virtue, even if it were only once in his whole life. The sexual act, successfully performed, was rebellion. Desire was thoughtcrime. Even to have awakened Katharine, if he could have achieved it, would have been like a seduction, although she was his wife.

But the rest of the story had got to be written down. He wrote:

> *I turned up the lamp. When I saw her in the light—*

After the darkness the feeble light of the paraffin lamp had seemed very bright. For the first time he could see the woman

CHECK THE FILM

Michael Radford's film *1984* (1984) presents this scene visually, but without the lengthy insight into Winston's mind which Orwell is able to give. Which do you feel to be the more powerful account?

properly. He had taken a step towards her and then halted, full of lust and terror. He was painfully conscious of the risk he had taken in coming here. It was perfectly possible that the patrols would catch him on the way out: for that matter they might be waiting outside the door at this moment. If he went away without even doing what he had come here to do—!

It had got to be written down, it had got to be confessed. What he had suddenly seen in the lamplight was that the woman was *old*. The paint was plastered so thick on her face that it looked as though it might crack like a cardboard mask. There were streaks of white in her hair; but the truly dreadful detail was that her mouth had fallen a little open, revealing nothing except a cavernous blackness. She had no teeth at all.

He wrote hurriedly, in scrabbling handwriting:

> *When I saw her in the light she was quite an old woman, fifty years old at least. But I went ahead and did it just the same.*

He pressed his fingers against his eyelids again. He had written it down at last, but it made no difference. The therapy had not worked. The urge to shout filthy words at the top of his voice was as strong as ever.

? **QUESTION**

Do you agree that **stereotypical** representation of women in the novel is a problem for the modern reader?

Winston is using his diary to develop both a sense of reality and an individual identity which are different from those laid down by the Party. He focuses on moments of his life which provoke strong feelings and reflects on what those feelings really are and on what the implications of each episode may be. The hesitation with which Winston writes about this particular event, breaking off to think about it, then finally hastening to set down the truth as quickly as possible, shows the depth of his embarrassment and horror. Although we are reading a third-person narrative, the **rhetorical questions** ('Why did it always have to be like this?') and the reflections which follow them allow us to hear what is passing through Winston's mind.

In itself the episode makes clear that the way of life which the Party imposes on its members is against human nature. (This may of course be true of all civilisations, in which case the Party's moral code could be interpreted as a **satire** on societies and religions in general.) After reading of Winston's frustration and loneliness, we are more able to understand the significance of his affair with Julia, which asserts natural human feeling against the Party's fanaticism.

However, we may also develop some reservations about Winston himself. His firm conclusion that 'The women of the Party were all alike' in their frigidity may at this stage sound almost like a fact, but it is firmly disproved when he meets Julia. His experiences have led him to a false conclusion, just as they will do at a later stage when he learns to love Big Brother. In the light of such misconceptions, we must wonder whether Winston's accounts of Katharine and the prostitute are any more accurate. After all, we do not hear their side of the story. Can we be sure Katharine's body was 'frozen' by the Party, rather than by her relationship with Winston? Winston compares the prostitute's face to a cardboard mask and her mouth to a cavern; how did she feel about him, an elite member of the Party, exploiting her poverty to obtain sexual relief?

In forcing himself to relive his experiences, Winston demonstrates to us how much courage is needed to set aside conventional thinking and face reality. Unfortunately for him, this process proves to be totally reversible. He conceives of his diary writing as a kind of mental therapy, by which he tries, unsuccessfully, to vent the frustrations and obsessions with which he cannot live. O'Brien will make the same claim for his conversion, telling Winston he is 'mentally deranged' (Part Three, Chapter 2, p. 258) and that his 'defective memory' needs to be adjusted until he is brought into a sane contact with reality.

CONTEXT

Many feminist critics, such as Beatrix Campbell, Deanna Madden and Daphne Patai, have voiced reservations about Orwell's depiction of women. Do you think this episode confirms their criticisms?

TEXT 2 – PART TWO, CHAPTER 10 (PP. 230–2)

'We are the dead,' he said.

'We are the dead,' echoed Julia dutifully.

'You are the dead,' said an iron voice behind them.

They sprang apart. Winston's entrails seemed to have turned into ice. He could see the white all round the irises of Julia's eyes. Her face had turned a milky yellow. The smear of rouge that was still on each cheekbone stood out sharply, almost as though unconnected with the skin beneath.

'You are the dead,' repeated the iron voice.

'It was behind the picture,' breathed Julia.

'It was behind the picture,' said the voice. 'Remain exactly where you are. Make no movement until you are ordered.'

It was starting, it was starting at last! They could do nothing except stand gazing into one another's eyes. To run for life, to get out of the house before it was too late – no such thought occurred to them. Unthinkable to disobey the iron voice from the wall. There was a snap as though a catch had been turned back, and a crash of breaking glass. The picture had fallen to the floor, uncovering the telescreen behind it.

'Now they can see us,' said Julia.

'Now we can see you,' said the voice. 'Stand out in the middle of the room. Stand back to back. Clasp your hands behind your heads. Do not touch one another.'

They were not touching, but it seemed to him that he could feel Julia's body shaking. Or perhaps it was merely the shaking of his own. He could just stop his teeth from chattering, but his knees were beyond his control. There was a sound of trampling boots below, inside the house and outside. The yard seemed to be full of men. Something was being dragged across the stones. The woman's singing had stopped abruptly. There was a long, rolling clang, as though the washtub had been flung across the yard, and then a confusion of angry shouts which ended in a yell of pain.

'The house is surrounded,' said Winston.

'The house is surrounded,' said the voice.

He heard Julia snap her teeth together. 'I suppose we may as well say good-bye,' she said.

'You may as well say good-bye,' said the voice. And then another quite different voice, a thin, cultivated voice which Winston had the impression of having heard before, struck in:

CONTEXT

The sudden arrest by secret police was a familiar feature of the 1930s, especially in Soviet Russia and Nazi Germany. The treatment of those accused in the novel particularly recalls that in Russia, where from 1936 the dictator Stalin held 'show trials' in which his victims confessed to treachery, often claiming that they had worked for a secret movement like the Brotherhood, led by his rival Leon Trotsky.

'And by the way, while we are on the subject, "Here comes a candle to light you to bed, here comes a chopper to chop off your head!"'

Something crashed onto the bed behind Winston's back. The head of a ladder had been thrust through the window and had burst in the frame. Someone was climbing through the window. There was a stampede of boots up the stairs. The room was full of solid men in black uniforms, with iron-shod boots on their feet and truncheons in their hands.

Winston was not trembling any longer. Even his eyes he barely moved. One thing alone mattered: to keep still, to keep still and not give them an excuse to hit you! A man with a smooth prizefighter's jowl in which the mouth was only a slit paused opposite him, balancing his truncheon meditatively between thumb and forefinger. Winston met his eyes. The feeling of nakedness, with one's hands behind one's head and one's face and body all exposed, was almost unbearable. The man protruded the tip of a white tongue, licked the place where his lips should have been and then passed on. There was another crash. Someone had picked up the glass paperweight from the table and smashed it to pieces on the hearth-stone.

As we read this section of the book, caught up in the story, and anxious to learn what will happen next, we do not stop to ask questions. If we did, we might wonder why the Thought Police have installed a telescreen where it might so easily be found, why they storm the house when they could have crept in and caught their victims unawares, and why they accompany their arrest with a jeering commentary. The answer is that it makes for a far more dramatic scene. It has to happen because this kind of shocking, violent arrest is what Winston and the reader have feared ever since the diary was first begun. After the extracts from Goldstein's book have enabled us to step back and reflect on totalitarianism with detachment, as an interesting idea to be viewed from a number of intellectual points of view, we suddenly find ourselves immersed in the experience of it. The episode makes plain the horror of living in a world where you may be violently and unjustly arrested at any moment, and in these terms it is certainly successful.

 CHECK THE FILM

Michael Radford's film *1984* (1984) follows the novel closely in this scene. As the events are so dramatic, Winston's first-person narrative is missed less than it is elsewhere in the adaptation.

The mocking voice which echoes the couple's statements could be considered unconvincing and 'stagey'. However, it changes the tone of the story in a striking way. The repetition creates a patterned feeling to the episode which makes the events seem suddenly strange. The disruptive effect is reinforced by the incongruous quotation from 'Oranges and lemons'.

The description of the voice as 'iron' characterises it as mechanical, inhuman and too firm to be resisted. This **metaphor** links it with the 'iron-shod' boots of the troopers (p. 231). The truncheon-wielding forces of Big Brother are described using violent verbs: 'flung', 'thrust', 'burst', 'smashed'. They are dark, hard and invulnerable, contrasting with the couple's soft bodies, which are pale with fear, 'milky yellow' skin housing entrails cold as 'ice', and with the fragile glass paperweight, **symbol** of privacy and subtle, personal feeling, which, like the window by which the men enter, is soon contemptuously broken.

As usual, the reader follows Winston's thoughts from moment to moment, and so empathises with him. We share his feelings through **free indirect discourse** ('it was starting at last!', p. 230) and share his desperate attempts to control his shaking body, then to avoid acting in a way which might provoke the trooper. We also share Winston's confusion about whom the iron voice belongs to, since the information is never stated clearly. However, we can infer from the 'different voice' the truth that Winston is too shaken to deduce, that it is Mr Charrington. When Charrington enters at the end of the chapter, our deduction is confirmed and Winston's perception catches up with ours, bringing Part Two to a firm conclusion. We then turn fearfully to Part Three, knowing that Winston and Julia now face the most terrible ordeal.

TEXT 3 – PART THREE, CHAPTER 3 (PP. 278–80)

Winston shrank back upon the bed. Whatever he said, the swift answer crushed him like a bludgeon. And yet he knew, he *knew*, that he was in the right. The belief that nothing exists outside your own mind – surely there must be some way of demonstrating that it was false? Had it not been exposed long ago as a fallacy? There was even a name for it, which he had

CONTEXT

Orwell considered calling the novel *The Last Man in Europe*.

forgotten. A faint smile twitched the corners of O'Brien's mouth as he looked down at him.

'I told you, Winston,' he said, 'that metaphysics is not your strong point. The word you are trying to think of is solipsism. But you are mistaken. This is not solipsism. Collective solipsism, if you like. But that is a different thing: in fact, the opposite thing. All this is a digression,' he added in a different tone. 'The real power, the power we have to fight for night and day, is not power over things, but over men.' He paused, and for a moment assumed again his air of a schoolmaster questioning a promising pupil: 'How does one man assert his power over another, Winston?'

Winston thought. 'By making him suffer,' he said.

CHECK THE FILM

In Michael Radford's *1984* (1984) O'Brien is played by the noted actor Richard Burton, who gives the part a quiet, relentless authority in what was one of his last, and perhaps best, performances.

'Exactly. By making him suffer. Obedience is not enough. Unless he is suffering, how can you be sure that he is obeying your will and not his own? Power is in inflicting pain and humiliation. Power is in tearing human minds to pieces and putting them together again in new shapes of your own choosing. Do you begin to see, then, what kind of world we are creating? It is the exact opposite of the stupid hedonistic Utopias that the old reformers imagined. A world of fear and treachery and torment, a world of trampling and being trampled upon, a world which will grow not less but *more* merciless as it refines itself. Progress in our world will be progress towards more pain. The old civilisations claimed that they were founded on love or justice. Ours is founded upon hatred. In our world there will be no emotions except fear, rage, triumph and self-abasement. Everything else we shall destroy – everything. Already we are breaking down the habits of thought which have survived from before the Revolution. We have cut the links between child and parent, and between man and man, and between man and woman. No one dares trust a wife or a child or a friend any longer. But in the future there will be no wives and no friends. Children will be taken from their mothers at birth, as one takes eggs from a hen. The sex instinct will be eradicated. Procreation will be an annual formality like the renewal of a ration card. We shall abolish the orgasm. Our neurologists are at work upon it now. There will be no loyalty, except loyalty towards the Party. There will be no love, except the love of Big Brother. There will be no laughter, except the laugh of triumph over a defeated enemy. There will be no art, no literature, no science. When we are omnipotent we shall have no more need of science. There will be no distinction between beauty and ugliness. There will be no curiosity, no enjoyment of the process of life. All competing pleasures will be destroyed. But always – do not forget this, Winston – always there will be the intoxication of power, constantly increasing and constantly growing subtler. Always, at every moment, there will be the thrill of victory, the sensation of trampling on an enemy who is helpless. If you want a picture of the future, imagine a boot stamping on a human face – for ever.'

Although none of us will have been in a situation quite as terrifying as Winston's, we have all been in analogous situations, intimidated into listening and agreeing with someone to whom we are opposed. Orwell even supplies one comparison by noting that O'Brien has the 'air of a schoolmaster questioning a promising pupil' (p. 279), one, that is to say, he hopes will absorb the views which he is given and adopt them as his own. O'Brien is a far more powerful character than we shall ever meet in our own experience, however, not only because of the physical pain he can inflict on his victim, but because he is able to look into Winston's mind and respond to his very thoughts. This is not a **realistic** ability, but the purpose of the book is to expose the mentality behind totalitarianism as plainly and forcefully as possible. The scenes in the Ministry of Love may not be wholly plausible, but they are not easily forgotten; nor is the vision of relentless evil which they convey.

To Winston, O'Brien's ideas are 'like a bludgeon', as much a weapon against the freedom of the individual as are the truncheons carried by the Thought Police troopers (p. 278). This does not make O'Brien's arguments true or even convincing, although he states them with such confidence that, like Winston, we may for a time be cowed into thinking that they have substance. O'Brien's speech is in fact a skilful piece of **rhetoric**, proceeding from opinions to speculation in a series of confident, rhythmic statements, interspersed with **rhetorical questions**. Key words like 'power'

CHECK THE BOOK

Patrick Reilly in his essay '1984: The Insufficient Self' (in his book The Literature of Guilt: From Gulliver to Golding, 1988) points out that, because we accept Winston as our 'spokesman' earlier in the book, we are put in a challenging position when he is defeated. 'The book asks us to identify with Winston and to say honestly how we would fare in his place.'

and 'no' are repeated forcefully. Parallel sentence structures are employed to intensify the rhythm and the sense of inevitability: 'There will be no ... except ...' References to the listener draw him silently into the discourse: 'do not forget this, *Winston* ... If *you* want a picture of the future ...' (my italics, p. 280). Finally the **image** of a boot stamping on a face seals the speech with a vivid **metaphor** which sums up its meaning.

CHECK THE BOOK

Christopher Hitchens in *Orwell's Victory* (2002) claims that '*Nineteen Eighty-Four* is the only English contribution to the literature of twentieth-century totalitarianism able to stand comparison with Silone and Koestler and Serge and Solzhenitsyn.'

Advances made in biological science over the last half-century may cause O'Brien's vision of sexual modification to seem more plausible than they would have appeared in 1949, but it is likely that Orwell's original intention was for the passage to be the ranting of a madman. O'Brien's goals of abolishing the orgasm, along with art and science, and removing the distinction between beauty and ugliness, are so preposterous that they totter on the boundary between horror and humour. The faintest suspicion that O'Brien might be right is enough to disturb us, but the really frightening aspect of his ideas is that he himself believes them and is ready and able to act on them, while there is nothing that Winston can do to change his mind or resist because the traditions of liberty have been wiped away, leaving him no source of resistance except whatever conviction and courage he can find within himself.

CRITICAL APPROACHES

CHARACTERISATION

The characters in *Nineteen Eighty-Four* are straightforward ones, with the partial exception of the central character, Winston Smith. While this may disappoint readers who value rich, developed characters in fiction, it cannot be considered a flaw in this particular kind of book, for by its nature a **science fictional dystopia** sets out to dramatise ideas rather than personalities. Indeed one of Orwell's key points is that a world which was as centrally controlled and hostile to individualism as '1984' would have to eliminate anyone who possessed originality in order to maintain its existence.

WINSTON SMITH

Winston is a smallish, frail figure, who wears the compulsory blue Party uniform. He is thirty-nine years old with fair hair and a red face, and has a varicose ulcer above his right ankle. Employed at the Ministry of Truth to rewrite the records of the past, he comes to realise that the unrevised past which he is burying was a better world than the present. He starts writing a diary in order to try to think for himself and later develops a relationship with Julia which he finds nourishes both spirit and body. Having managed to unlearn some of the assumptions of a Party intellectual, he comes to value the way of life of the lower-class proles. However, he remains isolated in his rebellion, since he receives little intellectual support from Julia, is unable to achieve any meaningful contact with the proles and is betrayed when he attempts to join the Brotherhood. Once he has been arrested and reduced to a single, fearful rebel against the system, his conviction that he is right and the Party wrong is not strong enough to withstand torture and brainwashing.

Winston's surname establishes him as an everyman figure, but his first name is more open in its implications. Some of today's readers, knowing Winston to be a name favoured by West Indians, might assume that he is black (which would give an additional twist to the chess metaphor in the final chapter), but the intended reference is

QUESTION

How effectively does Orwell depict character in the novel?

clearly to Winston Churchill, Britain's prime minister during the Second World War. The most straightforward interpretation of this link is that, like his namesake, Winston Smith represents resistance to evil. However, his first name could also be interpreted as an **ironic** comment on his lack of fitness to resist evil, contrasting him with Churchill, or even as a **satirical** reflection on how, under Churchill's leadership during the Second World War, government controls had increased.

? QUESTION

Compare and contrast the novel and Michael Radford's 1984 film version of the story, investigating the reasons for their differences.

The story of *Nineteen Eighty-Four* is almost entirely Winston's story. Everything that happens in it happens in relation to him. It begins with the first of his diary entries, then traces each stage of his rebellion until his final capitulation. The narrative is focused on him throughout, allowing us to share not only his reflections but also his dreams and longings. We observe his personality begin to grow as memories of the past force themselves back and he starts to come to terms with his feelings about his lost mother. Ultimately, however, such development is brought to a brutal end and his growing self is replaced by a superficial conformist personality imposed from outside.

Paradoxically, although our main impression of Winston is that he is a powerless victim of an evil world, it also seems to be a world which manifests his inner feelings, almost as if he is dreaming it into being. There are several occasions when his dreams come true, from his liaison with Julia in the Golden Country to his exposure to the rats in Room 101. We are told from the beginning that he foresees the fatal outcome of his rebellion. It sometimes seems that part of him wants to be 'cured', perhaps as an escape from, or punishment for, the guilt which he feels over his childhood selfishness.

Because we share Winston's ideas and perceptions so fully, it is easy to assume that we are always intended to sympathise and agree with him. However, as the book progresses, the reader is likely to notice that Winston's views are not always reliable. Winston's perceptions of his wife Katharine and the proles, for example, are so **stereotypical** that they invite scepticism. His prediction that Parsons will never be arrested proves false and, remarkably, he fails to notice any of the sinister clues about Charrington or O'Brien.

Far from being an admirable character, Winston considers murdering his wife, vows to kill children when being sworn into the Brotherhood and eventually betrays Julia. Although he desires to behave with decency, his environment repeatedly inhibits him from doing so. As for love, his only real experience of it is the love which his mother gave him in his childhood. His relationship with Julia is quite limited in comparison. We never see him idealise her or put her interests before his own, so why should we be surprised when he is terrorised into betraying her?

Orwell certainly expects us to retain some **distance** from Winston's point of view. In the first chapter when Winston scribbles his initial diary entry, expressing normal Party attitudes towards the violent film and the prole woman, we can see that this is only his training speaking, just as in the final paragraph of the book we discount his love for Big Brother as the result of brainwashing. In between these two points, however, the reader has to exercise personal judgement about which of Winston's sentiments to accept and which to reject.

JULIA

Julia, whose last name we never know, is introduced in the first chapter. At this stage Winston suspects her of being a spy, and this possibility remains throughout the book. Evidence for her membership of the Thought Police is noted in the commentaries to the chapters and, if we break off from the experience of reading and think about it with detachment, it is quite powerful evidence. We should remember, however, that the book has several unrealistic features which create a sense of entrapment and their effect has to be judged from the reading experience, not from a detached analysis. Most readers have accepted the relationship between Julia and Winston as authentic, and found their subdued meeting in the final chapter a moving conclusion.

Julia is a bold-looking twenty-six-year-old, with thick, dark hair, a freckled face and athletic movements. She wears a scarlet sash which appears to demonstrate her support for the Party's Anti-Sex League but which she actually wears in order to make herself more sexually attractive. Under pretence of conformity, she is a promiscuous disbeliever in the Party's moral code. She works, appropriately

? QUESTION

How do you evaluate Julia? Is she a heroine, a stereotypical sex object, or perhaps a double agent pretending to be both?

enough, in the Fiction Department. As her oily hands suggest, she is a highly practical person, skilfully organising love affairs and obtaining luxury goods from her admirers. Although she does not regard revolution against the system as a realistic option, her affection for Winston leads her to support him in his attempt to join the Brotherhood. Sometimes her cynicism enables her to see reality more clearly than he does, as when she suggests that the Party may be bombing its own people in order to foment hatred of the enemy.

It is arguable that in some respects Julia is a male fantasy figure. While a girl who likes to enjoy herself is plausible enough, a girl who flings herself determinedly at a downtrodden older man, arranges their meetings and takes charge of their sex life is rather less so. Orwell introduces her largely to help Winston create an alternative life for himself and to act as a sounding board for his ideas. The stages of his rebellion are matched by his reactions to her. She is glimpsed only briefly in Part One, in Part Two she becomes his lover, then she is absent from Part Three until the end, where the 'converted' Winston shows that he no longer has any feelings for her. Throughout, she receives limited character development in her own right.

O'BRIEN

O'Brien is a member of the Inner Party. He too is introduced in the first chapter. He has the build of a prizefighter, burly and thick-necked, with a coarse, humorous, brutal face, but habitually readjusts his glasses on his nose in a way which suggests a contrasting urbanity and intellect. From the start Winston longs to talk to him, feeling instinctively that such a man would not be bound by orthodox thinking and would therefore understand him. He even links O'Brien to the voice in one of his dreams. Eventually O'Brien offers to induct him into the Brotherhood, but does so only to entrap him.

The danger should have been evident to Winston when O'Brien was able to recognise two of his pet phrases just as though he had been spying on him. When they meet again for the interrogation, O'Brien actually seems able to read Winston's mind. Like the evidence which suggests that Julia is a member of the Thought Police, O'Brien's

QUESTION

It is surprising that no one has suggested a gay reading of *Nineteen Eighty-Four*. Do you think that in a sense Winston loves and needs O'Brien more than he does Julia?

telepathic powers are not perhaps to be taken in their own right, but understood as a method by which Orwell creates a sense of Winston's vulnerability. We learn finally that O'Brien is no mere torturer but a kind of religious inquisitor, a fanatic whose aim is to convert his victims to orthodoxy before he executes them.

OTHER PARTY MEMBERS

All of the other members of the Party are simple **stereotypes**, introduced to contrast with Winston, to convey information and to help advance the **plot**. Parsons is an enthusiastic obsessive who supports the Party without reservations, Syme a haughty intellectual, Ampleforth a vapid poet. Bumstead and the cadaverous man he tries to help are victims of torture who have contrasting attitudes or who are perhaps merely at different stages of their destruction. Mrs Parsons is a downtrodden housewife, the Parsons children aggressive brats and Charrington a refined elderly prole who turns out to be a member of the Thought Police in disguise.

THE PROLES

The proles are introduced in Part One, Chapter 1 through the woman in the cinema, a positive figure in her values yet a stereotypical figure of fun in her behaviour: a loud, disruptive character who can only express herself in repetitive and common language. A similarly limited impression is made by other proles later in the book: the slum-dwellers and pub-goers of Part One, Chapter 8; the woman at the clothes line in Part Two, Chapters 4 and 9; and the prostitute in Part Three, Chapter 1. They are not developed characters, but figures from a comic postcard or a music hall sketch. Although Winston eventually comes to respect the proles for their vitality and their humane perspective which contrasts with the Party's world-view, they are presented as mental inferiors who have not consciously rejected the Party's vision, but are simply incapable of understanding it. For this reason they are also incapable of challenging the Party and creating a world which would do their values justice.

Many critics have found the proles unconvincing and have condemned them as stereotypes. They argue that Orwell, the

 CHECK THE BOOK

In *Modern Masters: Orwell* (1971) Raymond Williams strongly criticises Orwell's depiction of working-class people.

product of upper-class schools and a formative period spent as an imperial policeman in Burma, could not empathise adequately with those below him in the class structure. This is a plausible argument, but we should also consider the possibility that it rests on a misunderstanding of Orwell's intention. Like the sudden switch of enemy from Eurasia to Eastasia, or the conversion of the English language into Newspeak, the way of life of the proles may be a feature of the book which is not meant to be **realistic**, but a **satirical** exaggeration which dramatises a point, in this case the damage done by class divisions. In his introduction to the 1989 Penguin edition of the book, Ben Pimlott suggests that Orwell may be mocking the sentimental faith which some socialists have in 'the people', challenging them to explain what makes their prediction of a workers' revolution more likely than this vision of perpetual oppression.

We should also remember that Winston is not an entirely reliable narrator. He is a Party member who never entirely succeeds in freeing himself from the Party's world-view. The question of how widespread resistance may be, particularly whether the Brotherhood really exists, is left open. When O'Brien assures Winston that the proles can't rebel, he says, 'I do not have to tell you the reason: you know it already' (Part Three, Chapter 3, p. 274), but we do not have to accept the Party line which both of them share.

THEMES

The fundamental theme of the book is the conflict between the individual and the social system. It is a theme with which many people find it easy to identify. We all sometimes feel isolated in a world which seems determined to thwart our needs, deny our perceptions and foist false values upon us. In *Nineteen Eighty-Four* this feeling is cast into a fantastic form and pursued to a horrifying extreme.

While this ease of identification is a major source of the book's appeal, it is the particular nature of the nightmare world Winston inhabits which accounts for the enormous impact that the book has

CHECK THE NET
The Chestnut Tree Café web site features many thematic articles on Orwell and *Nineteen Eighty-Four*. Look for these at **http://www. netcharles.com**

had. Winston's rebellion is not directed simply against a repressive job or unsympathetic parents, but an infinitely more alarming antagonist, totalitarianism. Many of the book's original readers, having witnessed the relentless mass cruelty unleashed by Hitler and Stalin, naturally asked themselves whether such a system could ever develop in their own countries. It was undeniable that throughout the first half of the twentieth century there had been more and more government intervention in people's lives in all developed nations, and that this trend had been accelerated by the Second World War. Orwell believed that greater government power was not only inevitable but was the only practicable way to bring about a more equal and democratic society, yet he feared that it could all too easily end in totalitarianism, a closed society where everything and everyone was controlled by a rigid dictatorship. The best way to avoid the danger was for people to be aware of the problem and vigilant in ensuring that it did not come about. *Nineteen Eighty-Four* was written to assist in this task.

Orwell takes some of the worst features of Nazi Germany and Communist Russia, imagines them refined to a vicious perfection by time and improved technology, and projects them onto the Britain of the near future, giving us an alarming reading experience which will encourage us to oppose this evil, plus a clear model of what it is that we should oppose. The book makes it clear that the power of totalitarianism does not derive simply from the power of the state, immense though that may be, but also from the weakness of the citizens. While the proles are victims because they are uninterested in politics and accept government as they do the weather, intellectuals like Winston are contrastingly vulnerable to the impressive-sounding philosophical arguments which the rulers use to justify their power and to the pseudo-religious promise that, in joining them, individuals will be accepted into a protecting order, freed from the anxiety, guilt and weakness which are actually a normal part of the human condition.

While totalitarianism is Orwell's chief target, *Nineteen Eighty-Four* also conveys a suspicion of modern life in general. Much of what Orwell foresaw has since come into being – television, security cameras, the twenty-four-hour clock, metrication, the loss of

CHECK THE BOOK
Orwell discusses his motivation and themes in his essay 'Why I Write', which is included in *Essays* (1994) and other collections of his writings.

Britain's status as a great power – but so far without the sinister consequences which he linked to these developments. Orwell's scepticism towards modernity can still be defended, however, for a major theme of the book is the struggle of the individual to lead an authentic life, fully in touch with their feelings, in a 'packaged' world of media manipulation and social expectation. To Orwell the good life is only loosely linked to affluence and technology; it has far more to do with experiencing a meaningful occupation and satisfying relationships, with self-knowledge and closeness to the basic facts of life. The book suggests that future developments may bring into being social forces so powerful that they can cut off the individual from these sources of health and leave him or her a victim of manipulation from above. The form this alienating society can take may be a brutal one as in *Nineteen Eighty-Four* or a pleasure-obsessed, affluent one as in *Brave New World*, but the worry is the same, and arguably it is a concern which should not be lightly dismissed.

It is worth remarking, finally, on the themes which are absent from *Nineteen Eighty-Four*. Although Orwell was a socialist, the book contains no direct advocacy of socialism. The book shows a world full of hate, but has relatively little to say about love. The struggle for freedom and creativity is defeated; no hope offered. Those who conclude from this that the book expresses despair, perhaps because Orwell was dying when he wrote it, may have missed the point, however. The confrontation between Winston and O'Brien demonstrates how hard it is to prove what is right and wrong through mere verbal argument. Orwell surely expects us to supply from our own experience both the knowledge of what is at stake in our particular time and place and the passion to fight for what truly matters to us.

 CHECK THE BOOK

Chapter 5 of Malcolm Bradbury's *The Modern English Novel* (1993) describes the social and cultural features of the period.

LANGUAGE AND STYLE

Nineteen Eighty-Four has many of the stylistic virtues which Orwell developed in his non-fictional books and essays. The vocabulary is a plain one, with few unfamiliar words to get in the way of our understanding. When any new words have to be introduced, like 'Minitrue' and 'doublethink', their meaning is explained immediately. Figurative language is restrained and generally takes the form of simple, even commonplace **similes** which add helpful emphasis and connotation to what they describe. Victory Gin is 'like a dose of medicine' (Part One, Chapter 1, p. 7); that is to say, unpleasant but therapeutic. The Thought Police carry off Julia 'like a sack' (Part Two, Chapter 10, p. 232); she is reduced from an autonomous person to a mere object to be hauled away and emptied out. For moments when Winston's emotions are particularly intense, there are also **metaphors**, made more powerful by their sparing use: 'The paperweight was the room he was in, and the coral was Julia's life and his own, fixed in a sort of eternity at the heart of the crystal' (Part Two, Chapter 4, p. 154).

Orwell's writing voice – an apparently unassuming one, which prefers concrete to abstract nouns, a casual to a formal tone and short statements to long, and which seems to think through a topic step by step, sharing the process with the reader, sometimes breaking off to ask a question or describe something in a mocking way – is a highly effective one for leading us through an argument, but it is not necessarily well suited to the demands of fiction writing. The creation of a fictional world with credible characters requires more subtle language than is needed to put over a discussion, and it has been argued that this is a source of weakness in Orwell's early novels. However, because the central character of *Nineteen Eighty-Four* is himself a kind of journalist, preoccupied by the issues which interested Orwell, much of the book is able to incorporate the Orwell 'voice' in a wholly appropriate way. The 'voice' actually belongs to the narrator rather than to Winston, but echoes Winston's thoughts through the use of **free indirect discourse**.

Orwell varies the texture of the book by bringing in other language features to evoke the context in which Winston's thoughts are formed. The adjectives used in the descriptions are often sordid, emphasising the poverty of his environment. The Saint Pancras district is 'battered … filthy … narrow', housing people who are 'swollen waddling … old bent … ragged barefooted' (Part One, Chapter 8, p. 86). Many of the similes used refer to animals. This is a favourite device of Orwell's, reflecting his down-to-earth view

CHECK THE BOOK
Chapter 10 of Roger Fowler's *The Language of George Orwell* (1995) contains a thorough discussion of his language and style as they are developed in *Nineteen Eighty-Four.*

CHECK THE BOOK

Roger Fowler in Chapter 4 of *The Language of George Orwell* (1995) notes: 'In demotic English, animals are frequently the vehicles for abuse' but such comparisons are particularly one of 'Orwell's negative preoccupations'.

of life, but applied to people with a sinister outlook it acquires an additional **satirical** charge, as in the 'gorilla-faced guards' (Part One, Chapter 1, p. 6) and the 'small, swiftly-moving, beetle-like man' (Part Two, Chapter 1, p. 118).

Other **registers** increase the diversity of the book further. Some work well, others less so, but overall they ensure that, despite the constant emphasis on Winston's inner reflections, the language does not become monotonous. There are the state's propaganda slogans, so striking that some have become known even to people who have not read the book, such as the ambiguous 'Big Brother is watching you' (Part One, Chapter 1, p. 3), a threat which scarcely even pretends to offer reassurance, and the paradoxical 'Freedom is slavery' (Part One, Chapter 2, p. 29). There is the cheerful camaraderie of Julia ('Just let me show you what I've brought', Part Two, Chapter 4, p. 147), the mindless enthusiasm of Parsons ('Pretty smart for a nipper of seven, eh?', Part One, Chapter 5, p. 60) and the proles' cockney ('I arst you civil enough, didn't I?', Part One, Chapter 8, p. 91). The crude fumbling for meaning of Winston's early diary entries (*'theyll shoot me i dont care'*, Part One, Chapter 1, p. 21) contrasts with the fluent analyses of Goldstein ('In so far as the war has a direct economic purpose, it is a war for labour power', Part Two, Chapter 9, p. 194), the simplistic formulations of the history textbook (*'These rich men were called capitalists. They were fat, ugly men with wicked faces'*, Part One, Chapter 7, p. 76) and the aggressive sophistries of O'Brien ('We make the laws of Nature', Part Two, Chapter 3, p. 277). There are the two contrasting songs (the sentimental 'It was only an 'opeless fancy' and the sneering 'Under the spreading chestnut tree'), the nostalgic descriptions of nature ('the ground was misty with bluebells', Part Two, Chapter 2, p. 123) and the almost **surreal** nightmares which have an uncertain relation to the waking world ('Suddenly he floated out of his seat, dived into the eyes and was swallowed up', Part Three, Chapter 2, p. 255).

Above all, there is the most prominent and controversial aspect of the book's language, Newspeak – the official language of Oceania, intended to replace Standard English or Oldspeak around the year 2050. Some critics have objected that Newspeak is impossible.

Most of what we think does not take the form of words, they point out, and when we do use words to formulate our ideas, we are not controlled by them, but swap them around and substitute them until we are satisfied they make acceptable sense. How can a word be abolished? How can unofficial meanings be outlawed? How can natural language change and variation be prevented? Once again, however, Orwell is not making a prediction, but satirically exaggerating an important point. In 'Politics and the English Language' (1946) he had warned that careless language use, particularly over-reliance on ready-made phrases, can lead to careless and insensitive thinking. If people use **jargon** terms like 'elimination of unreliable elements' to describe murdering their opponents, then it is comparatively easy for them to avoid admitting the horror of their acts, even to themselves. The more such vague jargon there is in circulation, the easier it is to have sloppy thoughts. Newspeak makes us aware of the problem, but by developing it to the point of absurdity, it reminds us at the same time of the potential strength of Oldspeak, and how in the hands of great or even simply careful writers our existing language can be used to clarify our ideas and to extend and enrich our experience. If a translation of the Declaration of Independence consists simply of the word '*crimethink*', we may wonder what the works of 'Shakespeare, Milton, Swift, Byron, Dickens and some others' (Appendix, p. 325) will consist of when the likes of Ampleforth have finished with them.

In a world in which verbal language is being systematically corrupted, there is a counterbalancing emphasis in the book on body language, which often expresses feelings more openly, such as the 'magnificent gesture by which a whole civilisation seemed to be annihilated' when Julia strips herself and flings away her uniform (Part Two, Chapter 2, p. 131), the contorted motions of the Hate Week speaker who 'clawed the air menacingly' (Part Two, Chapter 9, p. 188) and, most important of all, the 'enveloping, protecting gesture' of Winston's mother when she puts her arm around his sister (Part Two, Chapter 7, p. 171) and the similar gesture 'made again thirty years later by the Jewish woman he had seen on the news film, trying to shelter the small boy from the bullets, before the helicopters blew them both to pieces' (Part Two, Chapter 7, p. 167).

CHECK THE BOOK

The first part of David Wykes's *A Preface to Orwell* (1987) contains a wide-ranging account of Newspeak.

CHECK THE BOOK

There is a good introduction to narrative techniques in Section 5 of *Ways of Reading: Advanced Reading Skills for Students of English Literature* by Martin Montgomery, Alan Durant, Nigel Fabb, Tom Furniss and Sarah Mills (1992).

NARRATIVE TECHNIQUES AND STRUCTURE

The story is a simple one, and is straightforwardly divided into three parts: a beginning, a middle and an end. It starts with Winston's decision to think for himself despite the likelihood that this will lead to his death. We are also in the first chapter introduced to Julia and O'Brien, and from the way that they are singled out we infer they will be significant characters. The remainder of Part One shows us the world in which Winston is trapped and his reactions to it. Part Two contains the rebellion. Winston has an illegal affair with Julia and through O'Brien the couple join the Brotherhood. The pair are then taken prisoner. Part Three recounts Winston's defeat.

The tale is narrated in the third person, but focused entirely on one character, Winston, whose point of view we occupy through **free indirect discourse** and also through his speech and diary entries. Only two other characters feature heavily in the book, O'Brien and Julia, and they are important purely because of what they mean to Winston. The book is therefore the exploration of a single consciousness. We are immersed in Winston's thoughts and feelings. We follow his experiences, held by the drama of his situation and fascinated by the world in which he is trapped, so like our own in some ways, but so unlike it in others.

One reason the book is disturbing is because, despite Winston's efforts, his consciousness is ultimately beyond his control, attacked not only from outside by propaganda and regulation, but from inside by nightmares and memories, over both of which O'Brien finally proves himself master. While the sensory world of the story seems to be a solid one, made out of such ingredients as dilapidated buildings, bad smells and poor-tasting food, Winston's consciousness frequently undergoes cinematic **dissolves** from the present to the past and from waking to dreaming. It would be no surprise, though it would be a big disappointment, if the book finally revealed itself to be the creation of a mental patient with O'Brien as his therapist. For all its surface **naturalism**, *Nineteen Eighty-Four* is a work of intense paranoid fantasy.

Winston is a victim of a conspiracy so thorough that the Thought Police themselves seem to have initiated his rebellion in order to be able to defeat it (putting him in a flat where he cannot always be seen by the telescreen, selling him the diary and so on), leaving him virtually no autonomy even as a rebel. What he dreams earlier in the book comes true at a later juncture. He dreams of seeing Julia taking off her clothes in the country; later it happens. He dreams of a voice like O'Brien's saying 'We shall meet in the place where there is no darkness' (Part One, Chapter 2, p. 27) and of 'a wall of darkness' behind which is something he dares not face (Part Two, Chapter 4, p. 151). When he uses the former phrase to O'Brien, the latter seems to recognise it and later introduces the rat torture by explaining to Winston that this is what his nightmare was really about. Similarly, Winston coins the phrase 'We are the dead' to describe the members of the Party, only to find it taken up, first by O'Brien when he describes the members of the Brotherhood, then by the Thought Police when he is taken prisoner.

The recurrence of these key phrases may detract from the book's **realism,** but by occurring at important moments and stressing points for our attention they help to give it shape. The same is true of other recurring features, such as the ominous children's rhyme 'Oranges and lemons', Winston's two visits to the Chestnut Tree Café and the use of **symbols** such as the dust which covers this uncared-for world, the clocks which regulate all activities, the **pastoral** golden country which Winston is able to enter only briefly, and the fragile paperweight which stands for everything that he wishes to attain. The appearance and reappearance of these **motifs** creates a strong sense that there are inevitable forces running beneath the events of the story. The motifs also give a slightly poetic quality to the book, helping to counterbalance the documentary texture caused by the enormous amount of plainly stated information which it contains.

The latter is sometimes cited as a problem. *Nineteen Eighty-Four* contains so much information that some readers find they cannot comfortably digest it all. In particular, the extracts from Goldstein's writing and the appendix on Newspeak have been accused of interrupting and distracting us from the story. The need to add these

> **CONTEXT**
>
> It is possible that Orwell derived the idea of the paperweight, which contains a piece of coral 'like a sugar rosebud' (Part Two, Chapter 10, p. 232), from Orson Welles's 1941 film *Citizen Kane*, where a similar paperweight is featured in the opening scene and is linked to the word 'Rosebud', symbolising Kane's lost innocence and happiness.

QUESTION

Do you agree with those critics who find the Newspeak appendix and the lengthy extracts from Goldstein's book to be a distraction from the story?

sections certainly shows that Orwell was not able to incorporate all of his ideas into the main narrative. Whether the result is clumsy or not is a matter of taste. Orwell himself certainly considered the passages of ideas essential and risked forty thousand pounds in royalties (far more in present-day money) by refusing to allow them to be cut in a US Book-of-the-Month Club edition.

SATIRE

The book directs contempt and ridicule at several targets. Most obviously, it is a **satire** on totalitarianism, largely modelled on Soviet Communism since at the time of writing this was the form which seemed to be most threatening. Orwell takes the typical features of totalitarian states and imagines them developed to new extremes. Big Brother is not just a dictator like Hitler or Stalin; he is an immortal ruler, a man-made god. Ingsoc does not just put forward one set of ideals while implementing another; it glories in its contradictions and boasts of them in slogans like 'Freedom is slavery' and concepts like 'doublethink'. The Party does not merely spy on its citizens and enforce conformity to its laws; it helps its members to betray it, so that it can then brainwash them and ensure they fully believe its lies. One effect of these extreme developments is to increase our understanding; we are able to see totalitarian features of society in a more dramatic form and so comprehend them more clearly. Another effect is to frighten us; we wonder whether such a society could really be brought about. Still another is to make us see the absurdity of totalitarian pretensions; we perceive their senselessness and, counterbalancing our fear, we find ourselves regarding them with amused contempt.

CHECK THE FILM

Satire is usually humorous. While the novel lacks obvious comedy, the comic potential of some of Orwell's ideas is developed, without loss of their horror, in Terry Gilliam's film *Brazil* (1985), a film which is based loosely on *Nineteen Eighty-Four* and makes an interesting comparison with it.

There are several religious references in the book's description of totalitarianism. This is hardly surprising, since one definition of totalitarianism is that it is the secularisation of religious aspirations, the attempt to create a heaven on earth. In the world of '1984' God is replaced by Big Brother. In the first chapter, during the Two Minutes Hate, a woman calls him her saviour and prays to him. The telescreen, correspondingly, is the all-seeing eye of God. The Party members are the saved, with O'Brien a religious inquisitor hunting down backsliding and heresy among them. The arch-heretic Goldstein has the first name Emmanuel, a biblical word for 'messiah' (Matthew 1:23). 'Thoughtcrime' is another word for sin, of which the wages is death. '2 + 2 = 5' is a miracle, which has to be accepted by an act of faith before one can be a true believer.

While a religious person would be entitled to interpret all this as satire against the secularisation of religious ideas, Orwell himself probably intended the satire to include certain features of organised religion, specifically Roman Catholicism, with its appeal to papal authority. In discussing the concept of 'blackwhite', Goldstein seems to echo the words of Ignatius Loyola, founder of the Jesuit order of priests, who said that his followers should believe white was black, and black white, if the Church required it. Orwell suggests in his essay 'Inside the Whale' (1940) that Catholicism and Communism have a similar appeal to disaffected intellectuals who want something to believe in, because both have a worldwide organisation, rigid discipline and power and prestige. However, Orwell's target is bigger than just Catholicism. He has in mind any use of religion as an excuse for one set of people to impose their wills on others, as can be seen from his sideswipe at Eastern religions under the name of 'Death-Worship' (Part Two, Chapter 9, p. 205).

CHECK THE BOOK
'Inside the Whale' is available in *Essays* (1994) and other collections of Orwell's writings.

Since *Nineteen Eighty-Four* is set in a Britain of the near future, Orwell naturally includes much satire on contemporary Britain, a world of shortages, rationing, nationalisation, bureaucracy, sexual repression and obsessive, hopeless gambling. (The lottery stands in for the football pools, though in 1995 Orwell's prophecy came true and the National Lottery replaced the pools as Britain's favourite form of gambling.) All of these targets are cast into a slightly unfamiliar form which tends both to clarify their nature and render them amusing.

Understandably, the story's setting in a world resembling post-war Britain led some readers to think the book's targets must also include the 1945–51 Labour government, which was nationalising important industries. Orwell firmly denied this, though he did admit that he was pointing out the danger of what the government

QUESTION

Do you think it is
necessary to have
an understanding
of the historical
background to the
novel in order for
us to appreciate
it as a work of
literature?

might one day become. (See **Social and political background** for
a more detailed account of this topic.) The point he consciously
intended to make was that totalitarianism was so powerful a trend,
even a genuinely constructive movement might be taken over by it.
However, some readers have felt that, if *Nineteen Eighty-Four* is an
attack on all kinds of totalitarianism, then it is up to them which
targets they choose to apply it to. Accordingly, the book has been
used as a political weapon in many countries, with members of
different parties accusing each other of putting forward 'Orwellian'
policies like those of 'Big Brother'. Arguably, this is the most
valuable dimension of Orwell's satire. By supplying us with a way
of naming the totalitarian threat, he has kept people aware of the
danger and so reduced the likelihood of it coming about.

PART FOUR

CRITICAL HISTORY

An enormous number of books about George Orwell and *Nineteen Eighty-Four* have been published, with an unsurprising surge of titles around the year 1984. The following account is not, therefore, comprehensive. In particular, it omits biographies, reference material, essays which are only available in journals and general studies of Orwell which do not offer any original insights into *Nineteen Eighty-Four*. (See **Further reading** for more details.)

Some general studies do shed light on the book by identifying themes and devices which link it to Orwell's earlier writings and to his personal experiences. In particular, many of them examine how Eric Blair developed 'George Orwell' as a literary persona with a characteristic set of attitudes and stylistic traits, and how he sought to reconcile the documentary, polemical approach which produced his outstanding books of the 1930s with the rather different requirements of his fiction writing. Among the most helpful of such overviews are *George Orwell: Fugitive from the Camp of Victory* by Richard Rees (1961), *The Crystal Spirit: A Study of George Orwell* by George Woodcock (1967), *The Making of George Orwell* by Keith Alldritt (1969), *Orwell and the Left* by Alex Zwerdling (1974), *A Reader's Guide to George Orwell* by Jeffrey Meyers (1975), *George Orwell: The Search for a Voice* by Lynette Hunter (1984) and *Modern Novelists: George Orwell* by Valerie Meyers (1991).

INTERTEXTUAL APPROACHES

Intertextual studies try to enhance understanding of *Nineteen Eighty-Four* by placing it in relation to other works, so that it is seen as part of an ongoing debate about twentieth-century politics and society.

Mark R. Hillegas's *The Future as Nightmare: H. G. Wells and the Anti-Utopians* (1967) and Krishan Kumar's *Utopia and Anti-Utopia in Modern Times* (1987) locate Orwell in the tradition of utopias and **dystopias**, the former from a literary standpoint, the latter from

 CHECK THE NET
A useful web site for further reading is **http://www. k-1.com/Orwell**, which includes biographical material, pictures, articles, Internet links and discussion boards, plus a range of Orwell's own essays.

a political one. Two books by Jenni Calder compare Orwell's work with that of writers who significantly influenced him: *Chronicles of Conscience: A Study of George Orwell and Arthur Koestler* (1968) and *Aldous Huxley and George Orwell: Brave New World and Nineteen Eighty-Four* (1976).

MARXIST CRITICISM

CHECK THE BOOK

The ideas of Karl Marx are helpfully explained and assessed in *Marx: A Very Short Introduction* by Peter Singer (1980).

Marxist critics, concerned with how literature has been shaped by class structure and social change, have tended to be attracted to Orwell because of his subject matter and themes but infuriated by the way he develops them. In *Modern Masters: Orwell* (1971) Raymond Williams suggests that the outlook of *Nineteen Eighty-Four* is far too negative because of Orwell's isolation as a ruling-class rebel, leading to a superficial and inadequate depiction, not only of the proles, but of personal relationships. *Inside the Myth: Orwell – Views from the Left* edited by Christopher Norris (1984) is a collection of essays by socialists questioning orthodox interpretations of Orwell from a wide variety of viewpoints, while *Orwell and the Politics of Despair: A Critical Study of the Writings of George Orwell* by Alok Rai (1988) is a more coherent and sympathetic socialist critique.

FEMINISM

Just as Marxists question the depiction of Ingsoc and the proles, so feminists challenge the representation of women in the book and the 'patriarchal' values which they claim it endorses. Examples of this are Beatrix Campbell's 'Orwell – Paterfamilias or Big Brother?' in Norris (1984), reprinted in Holderness, Loughrey and Yousaf (1998), and Deanna Madden's 'Women in Dystopia' in Katherine Anne Ackley, ed., *Misogyny in Literature: An Essay Collection* (1992). The most thoroughgoing feminist treatment of *Nineteen Eighty-Four* is in *The Orwell Mystique: Study in Male Ideology* by Daphne Patai (1984), which sees O'Brien as playing a power game with Winston according to traditional masculine rules which Julia attempts to subvert, but which Orwell himself finally endorses.

PSYCHOLOGICAL APPROACHES

Several critics have suggested that the ultimate coherence of Orwell's work is not to be found in either its political message or its aesthetic form, but the psychology of its author. Anthony West's influential essay 'George Orwell', in his *Principles and Persuasions: The Literary Essays of Anthony West* (1958), proposes that the ultimate model for Oceania is the prep school which Eric Blair attended, the experience of which was so traumatic that it decisively shaped his later perceptions and ideas. Richard Smyer's *Primal Dream and Primal Crime: Orwell's Development as a Psychological Novelist* (1979) approaches *Nineteen Eighty-Four* as a psychological novel in which Winston undergoes an extreme version of the normal 'civilising process' through interaction with mother and father figures. Michael Carter in *George Orwell and the Problem of Authentic Existence* (1985) sees Orwell's political activity as an attempt to create an identity which would enable him to escape feelings of past guilt, with Winston's struggle as a fictional parallel to this. Replying to negative evaluations of the book, Erika Gottlieb's *The Orwell Conundrum: A Cry of Despair or Faith in the Spirit of Man?* (1992) presents *Nineteen Eighty-Four* as a successful combination of political **satire** and psychological portraiture. Psychological and political readings are also balanced in Laurence Porter's essay 'Psychomania versus Socialism in *Nineteen Eighty-Four*' (in Rose, 1992).

Several of the above studies conceive of Winston as going through a spiritual crisis, confronting the meaning of human existence in a way which either parallels or satirises religious thinking. Patrick Reilly explores this confrontation in *George Orwell: The Age's Adversary* (1986), some of which reappears in his *Nineteen Eighty-Four: Past, Present and Future* (1989). The influence of religious ideas on Orwell is the particular focus of *The Last Man in Europe: Essay on George Orwell* by Alan Sandison (1974), later revised as *George Orwell: After 1984* (1986), and *The Road to Miniluv: George Orwell, the State and God* by Christopher Small (1975).

Important discussions of *Nineteen Eighty-Four*, some of them extracted from the books already listed, occur in the following essay

? QUESTION

In what sense might the book be considered a religious, rather than a political, novel?

collections: *Twentieth-Century Interpretations of Nineteen Eighty-Four* edited by Samuel Hynes (1971), *George Orwell: A Collection of Critical Essays* edited by Raymond Williams (1974), *Modern Critical Interpretations*: *Nineteen Eighty-Four* edited by Harold Bloom (1986), *Critical Essays on George Orwell* edited by Bernard Oldsey and Joseph Browne (1986), *Modern Critical Views: George Orwell* edited by Harold Bloom (1987), *George Orwell: A Reassessment* edited by Peter Buitenhuis and Ira Nadel (1988), *The Revised Orwell* edited by Jonathan Rose (1992) and *New Casebooks: George Orwell* edited by Graham Holderness, Bryan Loughrey and Nahem Yousaf (1998).

RECENT APPROACHES

All the above approaches continue, but it is now less common to simply celebrate Orwell as a truth teller or condemn him as a fabricator of myths; it is more common to accept *Nineteen Eighty-Four* as a complex text which requires a complex response and place it in contexts which allow us to see it in new light. For example, John Rodden's 'On the Political Sociology of Intellectuals' (in Rose, 1992, reprinted in Holderness, Loughrey and Yousaf, 1998) contrasts the attitudes of Orwell with those of other literary intellectuals of his era, and W. J. West's *The Larger Evils: Orwell and the Roots of Nineteen Eighty-Four* (1992) examines in detail events in the 1940s which may have influenced the creation of '1984'.

Post-structuralist and deconstructionist approaches to literature challenge the apparent intentions of the author and reinterpret the significance of the text by examining, on the one hand, its relation to larger systems of meaning and, on the other hand, its internal coherence. Such radical-seeming approaches to *Nineteen Eighty-Four* can be found in Norris (1984) and in Alan Kennedy's essay 'The Inversion of Form' in Holderness, Loughrey and Yousaf (1998), but these examples do not so much yield fresh insights as repeat the psychological approach discussed above with some new **jargon**, denying the book's political content, then interpreting it from the standpoint of Freudian psychology.

 QUESTION

Two key sentences in *Nineteen Eighty-Four* are 'I love you' and 'He loved Big Brother'. To what extent is the book about love?

Arguably a more productive recent approach is the linguistic one, which looks both at Orwell's own use of language and at his theories about the political manipulation of language. A wide-ranging essay on the issues raised by Newspeak appears in the first part of *A Preface to Orwell* by David Wykes (1987). 'Fourteen Types of Passivity' by Daniel Kies (in Rose, 1992) examines how Orwell uses grammatical structures to make us perceive Winston as a victim. *The Language of George Orwell* by Roger Fowler (1995) is a detailed and often illuminating examination of the distinctive features of Orwell's style and of his ideas about the effects of language.

The collapse of East European Communism has led many commentators to wonder how Orwell's views might be applied in the twenty-first century or, to put it more negatively, how they can try to add weight to their own political opinions by claiming Orwell's authority for them. John Newsinger's *Orwell's Politics* (1999) undertakes a detailed investigation of Orwell's developing ideas. Christopher Hitchens's *Orwell's Victory* (2002) is a spirited attempt to defend Orwell against his various detractors which has provoked some controversy. It comes under attack, for example, in *The Betrayal of Dissent: Beyond Orwell, Hitchens and the New American Century* by Scott Lucas (2004), which attempts to revive Raymond Williams's reservations about Orwell in a new context (see **Marxist criticism**).

CHECK THE BOOK

Orwell's views on language are memorably summarised in 'Politics and the English Language', which is available in *Essays* (1994) and other collections of his writings.

PART FIVE

BACKGROUND

CHECK THE BOOK
Many biographers have produced detailed accounts of Orwell's life, including Bernard Crick, Michael Shelden, Peter Davison, D. J. Taylor and Gordon Bowker.

CHECK THE BOOK
Anthony West's essay 'George Orwell', in his *Principles and Persuasions: The Literary Essays of Anthony West* (1958), suggests boarding school may have influenced Orwell negatively and formed the ultimate basis for the world of Big Brother.

GEORGE ORWELL

The man who is remembered today as 'George Orwell' began life as Eric Blair on 25 June 1903 in Bengal, where his father was an official in the Opium Department of the Indian Civil Service. After being taken to England in 1904, he lived for many years in Henley-on-Thames with his mother and older sister Marjorie. Eric's father joined them on his retirement in 1912, only to go away again in 1917 until 1919 as an officer in the Great War.

Eric, after attending a local school, was sent to St Cyprian's, a private boarding school in Eastbourne, about which he later wrote a scathing essay, 'Such, Such were the Joys'. It has been suggested that his experiences of punishment and emotional manipulation here as a child between 1911 and 1916 supplied an early model for Winston's 're-education' in *Nineteen Eighty-Four*. After a term at Wellington College, Eric won a scholarship to Eton. He was there from 1917 to 1921 but, although he was an intelligent pupil who enjoyed writing for college magazines, he made little academic effort. He seems to have already developed his lifelong dislike of succeeding on conventional terms. He did not go to university, but instead joined the Indian Imperial Police in 1922 and served as an Assistant Superintendent in Burma. While in England on sick leave in 1927, he resigned from the service, partly due to the chest illness which dogged him all his life, but also because he was disillusioned with imperialism and wished to try his hand at becoming a writer.

Apparently seeking to quench feelings of guilt about his privileged position in society, as well as to find material for stories and articles, he lived among the poor and posed as a tramp both in France and England (he lived in Paris from 1928 to 1929), before moving on to a series of temporary jobs such as teaching and bookselling. In order to avoid embarrassment to his parents, he adopted the pen name George Orwell for his first book, an account of some of his experiences called *Down and Out in Paris and London* (1933).

Despite continuing ill health, he worked hard at his writing, producing three novels in as many years, each concerning a rebel against conventional society whose experiences to some degree paralleled his own.

In 1936 he was commissioned to write a book about the economically depressed industrial areas of northern England. The result, *The Road to Wigan Pier* (1937), was a vivid, thought-provoking account, but was also highly controversial in its presentation of working people (anticipating similar controversy over the proles in *Nineteen Eighty-Four*) and in its abusive criticisms of progressive intellectuals. During the writing of the book, Orwell (he now used the names Blair and Orwell almost interchangeably) married Eileen O'Shaughnessy, whom he had met while she was studying for an MA in psychology.

By the time the book appeared, the couple had gone to Spain to support the republican side in the Spanish Civil War. Orwell served with an anarchist militia on the Aragon front until, in May 1937, he was shot through the throat by a Fascist sniper. However, his life proved to be under threat from the left as well as the right, for the Spanish Communists were now turning on some of their former allies, dishonestly branding them Fascist collaborators and executing many of them. The Blairs were lucky to escape across the border to safety. Because most of the British magazines which supported the republican side accepted the Communists' version of events in the name of solidarity, they refused to publish Orwell's eyewitness accounts, a suppression which undoubtedly influenced his conception of the rewriting of history in *Nineteen Eighty-Four*. Orwell's normal publisher, Gollancz, declined even to consider his book on the Spanish Civil War. *Homage to Catalonia* (1938) eventually appeared through another publisher.

With his ill health badly aggravated by the bullet wound, Orwell went to Morocco to recuperate in a hot climate, the trip funded by an anonymous donation from a friend, and there worked on his fourth novel, *Coming Up for Air* (1939), generally regarded as his best piece of conventional fiction. Returning to England in 1939, he wrote a book of essays called *Inside the Whale* (1940). As well as the

 CHECK THE BOOK

Orwell gives a vivid account of his experiences in the Spanish Civil War in his book *Homage to Catalonia* (1938).

title piece which reflects on the role of the writer in the contemporary world, this comprised a perceptive, inspirational literary study, 'Charles Dickens', and a ground-breaking discussion of popular culture, 'Boys' Weeklies'.

Orwell had opposed British involvement in a further European war, regarding it as likely to be a battle between national ruling classes which could bring no benefit to ordinary people, but when the Second World War was declared he changed his mind, partly because he hoped the upheaval of war might have the effect of revolutionising the country. Rejected by the army as medically unfit, he instead contributed to the war effort by joining the Home Guard, writing a portrait of British society, *The Lion and the Unicorn* (1941), and becoming a radio producer and writer for the Indian section of the BBC's Eastern Service. His experiences here and Eileen's in the government's Censorship Department gave him insights into bureaucracy and the creation of propaganda which undoubtedly shaped his conception of the Ministry of Truth in *Nineteen Eighty-Four*. He produced an enormous amount of journalism during the war years, including radio talks, film reviews and articles. In 1943 he quit the BBC, and on health grounds the Home Guard too. He became literary editor of the left-wing Labour Party newspaper, *Tribune*, contributing a weekly column 'As I Please'. In June 1944 he and his wife adopted a son whom they christened Richard Blair.

Orwell was disturbed by the positive view of the Russian state presented by the British media after the USSR had been invaded by Germany and switched sides to the Allies. (This is clearly reflected in *Nineteen Eighty-Four*, in Oceania's swift changes of ally and the cynical propaganda which accompanies these.) He wrote his classic **satire** *Animal Farm* (1945) to highlight how terribly the Russian regime had betrayed its revolutionary aims. Most publishers were unwilling to be associated with a book which mocked one of Britain's chief allies. However, by the time it finally appeared in 1945, Russia was again seen as an enemy and the book became an international bestseller, particularly in the USA, which was increasingly gripped by fear of Communism.

CONTEXT

One year after it was published, *Nineteen Eighty-Four* had sold 50,000 copies in Britain and 360,000 in the USA.

The years after the Second World War thus brought unexpected fame and wealth to Orwell. However, his wife had died suddenly a few months before *Animal Farm* appeared and his own health remained very poor. He continued to write prolifically, another volume of essays appearing in 1946. In the same year he moved to a remote farmhouse on the island of Jura in the Hebrides, where he could lead a simple life and work undisturbed, partly cared for by his younger sister Avril. He continued working on *Nineteen Eighty-Four* both here and at a hospital near Glasgow, where he was treated for seven months for tuberculosis. As the book's title suggests, it was completed in 1948. The proofs were corrected in 1949 at a sanatorium in the Cotswolds. Terminally ill, Orwell was transferred to University College Hospital, London, where he married Sonia Brownell, editorial assistant on the magazine *Horizon*. He died on 21 January 1950.

Orwell's books are *Down and Out in Paris and London* (1933), *Burmese Days* (1934), *A Clergyman's Daughter* (1935), *Keep the Aspidistra Flying* (1936), *The Road to Wigan Pier* (1937), *Homage to Catalonia* (1938), *Coming Up for Air* (1939), *Inside the Whale* (1940), *The Lion and the Unicorn* (1941), *Animal Farm* (1945), *Critical Essays* (1946) and *Nineteen Eighty-Four* (1949). Several selections of his work were published after his death, the most extensive of these being *The Collected Essays, Journalism and Letters*, edited by Sonia Orwell and Ian Angus in four volumes (1968). A *Complete Works of George Orwell*, edited by Peter Davison in twenty volumes, was published between 1986 and 1996.

SOCIAL AND POLITICAL BACKGROUND

The origins of *Nineteen Eighty-Four* lie in the years 1914 to 1945, a period of two world wars linked by a major economic slump which one historian has labelled 'the Age of Catastrophe'. The era began with the Great War of 1914 to 1918, which killed over eight million people, more than thirteen million if consequences are included such as the Russian Revolution and the epidemics which raged through Europe's weakened population.

 CHECK THE NET

Search the Internet for Louis Menand's thoughtful account of Orwell's life and work.

CHECK THE BOOK

Eric Hobsbawm describes the period he calls 'the Age of Catastrophe' in Part One of his book *Age of Extremes: The Short Twentieth Century, 1914–1991* (1994). There is a similarly thoughtful and wide-ranging account in *Dark Continent: Europe's Twentieth Century* by Mark Mazower (1998).

As a schoolboy whose father had gone off to battle, Orwell supported the war enthusiastically. Later, when he realised how little the peace settlement had achieved, he became disillusioned both with the war itself and with the political system which had produced it. Many shared this disillusionment. The returning soldiers had been promised a 'land fit for heroes', but the European economies struggled to recover from the damage that had been done to them by the war and by the peace treaties. In the worst case, German money in 1923 was worth a million millionth of its value ten years before. Although life had begun to improve by the end of the decade, the Wall Street Crash in the USA threw world capitalism into a further recession. By 1933 almost two and a half million breadwinners were unemployed in Britain and the normal party political system had been replaced by a coalition government. Elsewhere extremist groups, the Italian Fascists under Mussolini and the German Nazis under Hitler, managed to deliver their nations a degree of order and prosperity, but only at a high cost in intolerance and aggression. To some people these regimes seemed to represent a vigorous new type of society, firmly directed by a heroic leader and based on racial 'purity', a type of society which was bound to overthrow the ailing and directionless democracies.

CHECK THE NET
Search the Internet for a brief but informative essay entitled 'The Age of Totalitarianism: Stalin and Hitler'.

Others who thought that capitalism had now run its course looked to socialism for an alternative. Socialists thought that the nation's wealth should be owned by the whole community. Some of the most radical socialists, the Communists, believed that such a profound change could only come about through violent revolution and took Soviet Russia as their model. The Russian leaders claimed that, by seizing power during the Great War and ruthlessly controlling the whole of society from the top, they had turned their country from a backward state into a major industrial nation. They dismissed as exaggeration the deaths and torture of millions under Stalin's leadership. If Communism had not yet delivered what it promised, either in terms of democracy or of a good standard of living, it was bound to do so eventually, so they claimed.

Many socialists, not just the Communists, believed that capitalism was currently in the process of destroying itself. They thought that competition for markets between imperial nations had led to the

Great War and that now the ruling classes would probably turn to Fascism and fight a Second World War among themselves. This would be followed by the final battle between Fascism and Communism. The Spanish Civil War of 1936 to 1939, in which one side was supported by the Fascists and the other by the Communists, was interpreted as the first skirmish in this conflict.

Orwell was a socialist who shared some of these assumptions and went to fight for the Spanish republic, but he was too sincere a rebel against authority to feel comfortable with the Communists' idea of an intellectual elite taking power on the workers' behalf. He wished to see the ordinary people themselves in control, and cherished the brief period of worker solidarity which he glimpsed while in Barcelona. Having almost been killed there by the Spanish Communists, he came to realise that Soviet Communism and Fascism were in many ways similar totalitarian systems, even if they gave opposite excuses for their behaviour. (In a book review of 1940 he wrote: 'The two regimes, having started from opposite ends, are rapidly evolving towards the same system – a form of oligarchical collectivism', a classification to which he returns in the title of Goldstein's book.) The resemblance between Communism and Fascism became widely recognised when in 1939 Russia and Germany made a pact to refrain from attacking one another in order to be free to invade their neighbours, which they rapidly proceeded to do, dividing up Poland between them.

When Germany suddenly reversed its policy and invaded Russia in 1941, hoping to catch the Soviets off guard, it was the Allies' turn to make friends with the Communist regime. Orwell could see that it was necessary to work with the Russian government, but he still found this situation disturbing. Retaining the socialist view that capitalism could easily mutate into Fascism, he mistrusted all governments, especially wartime ones which were controlling everything from what people could buy in the shops to what they could hear in the news. He wrote *Animal Farm* in order to remind people how cruelly the Russian government had reneged on socialism, but also to make them alert to any dictatorial tendencies in their own rulers. The book ends with the pigs (the Communist leaders) who have enslaved the other animals (the workers)

CHECK THE BOOK
Orwell's review of *The Totalitarian Enemy* by F. Borkenau was collected in the second volume of his *Collected Essays, Journalism and Letters* (published in four volumes in 1968) and has since been included in other collections.

CHECK THE BOOK

Animal Farm, Orwell's 1945 satire on the Russian Revolution, was the book that made him famous.

negotiating and arguing with the humans (the capitalist leaders). Orwell intended this as an allusion to the 1944 Teheran Conference, the first of several meetings which the Russian, British and American governments held to decide who was going to control which parts of the world after the war.

In a sense, *Nineteen Eighty-Four* begins where *Animal Farm* left off. The world has now been divided into power blocs and, using the excuse of continued international hostility, the governments who control these areas have held on to, and refined, their wartime powers of control. Orwell genuinely feared that this was a possibility, although he referred to an element of **parody** in *Nineteen Eighty-Four*, indicating that not all the features envisaged in the book are meant to be taken literally. Allowing for some **satirical** exaggerations, his prophecy did prove accurate in describing the fate of Eastern Europe, which for almost the next half-century was subject to totalitarian rule by regimes controlled by Russia. In the event, Western Europe and the USA did not go the same way, but Orwell had had enough experience of censorship and propaganda during the war years to fear that the potential was there.

As a socialist, Orwell himself advocated collectivism, though not of the oligarchical kind. He believed that only through the state taking wealth and power from the ruling class and redistributing it could society become more equal and just. He supported the Labour government of 1945, with its policies of nationalisation and rationing, and indeed thought they did not go far enough. Yet in attacking the collectivism of the Communists and Fascists, he ran the risk of seeming to side with the Conservatives under Winston Churchill. Churchill had warned in a radio broadcast of 1945 that Labour could not implement such policies as the creation of a National Health Service without introducing 'some form of Gestapo'. Even *Nineteen Eighty-Four*'s very first reader, Orwell's publisher Frederic Warburg, thought that the book might win the Tories a million votes at the next election and wondered whether Churchill might be persuaded to write a preface to his namesake's tale.

It is not surprising that some readers interpreted the book as an attack on the Labour government. The descriptions of a wrecked and impoverished London in the opening pages of the book are highly reminiscent of the late 1940s. Because Lend-Lease aid from America had now ceased, conditions were in some respects worse in 1949 than they had been during the war and there was widespread frustration at the country's failure to get back to normal. One indication of this feeling was the popular comedy film *Passport to Pimlico* (1949), which appeared in the same year as *Nineteen Eighty-Four* and was much appreciated for the way it satirised rationing and bureaucracy. In the context of this period, the book's original readers would have quickly realised that 'Victory Mansions' and 'Victory Gin' implied state housing and the nationalisation of distilleries, with the poor quality of the 'Victory' brand suggesting that state ownership is a bad thing. The triumph of Ingsoc (a contraction of 'English Socialism', just as 'Nazi' was of the 'National Socialist Party') has brought about a system resembling Russian Communism, with Three-Year Plans like the Soviet five-year ones and Party members forbidden to buy on the 'free market' (Part One, Chapter 1, p. 8).

Orwell tried several times to dissociate himself from this apparent rejection of socialism. In a letter of 1949 he declares:

> My recent novel is NOT intended as an attack on Socialism or on the British Labour Party (of which I am a supporter) but as a show-up of the perversions to which a centralised economy is liable and which have already been partly realised in Communism and Fascism … The scene of the book is laid in Britain in order to emphasise that the English-speaking races are not innately better than anyone else and that totalitarianism, *if not fought against*, could triumph anywhere.

For decades after its publication, however, the book was still interpreted by many on the political right wing as anti-socialist and by many on the left (who, curiously, seem to have accepted a resemblance between their policies and Big Brother's) as a betrayal. Perhaps today it is easier to see it as an attack against all forms of totalitarianism, which merely takes conditions at the time it was written as its natural 'jumping-off' point.

CHECK THE FILM
The film *Passport to Pimlico* (1949) is about a district of London which is able to escape government rationing and bureaucracy when some old documents show that it is not historically part of Britain but belongs instead to the Duchy of Burgundy.

After the Age of Catastrophe came what we might loosely call the era of the Cold War, though Orwell himself lived to see only the start of it. For most of the period 1945 through to 1989 he seemed to be an impressive prophet. States with features reminiscent of Oceania were to be found on several continents. Even in the liberal democracies, state power was greater than anyone could have imagined a few decades previously. As Goldstein's book predicts, there were several power blocs, notably those led by Russia and the USA, which did not dare use nuclear weapons but made use of wars in disputed countries to apply military pressure to each other.

CHECK THE BOOK

The collapse of Communism in Eastern Europe is explained and analysed in Chapter 11 of Mark Mazower's *Dark Continent: Europe's Twentieth Century* (1998). Christopher Hitchens in *Orwell's Victory* (2002) claims that North Korea, under its dictator Kim II Sung, and then his successor Kim Jong II, was and still is a society frighteningly like Oceania.

The fall of European Communism in 1989 seems to have opened a new phase of history, and few people now advocate old-style socialist control of the economy from the centre, but it is probably an error to think that as a result of this *Nineteen Eighty-Four* has irretrievably 'dated'. After all, there are still many one-party states in the world which aspire to control their citizens' lives in a way which would warm O'Brien's heart. There are still plenty of thinkers who argue that the individual human being is merely a product of larger forces and is therefore of little account. Language is still systematically abused by politicians, journalists and advertisers in order to manipulate emotion and distort truth. Improvements in surveillance technology continue to present problems for civil liberties. People still struggle to be their full selves in societies which deny their aspirations. Although *Nineteen Eighty-Four* may be less topical than it once was, it is hard to imagine a time when it will not be relevant to a large body of readers.

LITERARY BACKGROUND

Ever since the fourth century BC, when Plato wrote his *Republic*, authors have been sketching imaginary societies as a way of expressing their ideals of what the world should be like and challenging the assumptions and customs of their own day. The best-known book of this type is *Utopia* by Thomas More (1516) and, because of this, all such imaginary societies are now called utopias. The utopian tradition also includes what have come to be called **dystopias**, portraits of imaginary societies which are much worse than our own, devised in order to show up unhealthy values and warn against future developments. In the first half of the twentieth century H. G. Wells, one of Orwell's favourite writers, was the most influential creator both of utopias and dystopias. Orwell had been highly influenced by Wells in his **realistic** novels and in his thinking (even his pen name 'George Orwell' seems to echo 'Herbert George Wells'), so it is not surprising that he again followed Wells when he decided to warn readers against totalitarian trends in society through dystopian **science fiction**. Of all Wells's many books, *When the Sleeper Wakes* (1899), a tale set in a centrally controlled state in 2100, is the one with the most influence on *Nineteen Eighty-Four*, though the figure of O'Brien may also owe something to the sinister title character of a much better book by Wells, *The Island of Doctor Moreau* (1896). However, the chief sources for his book were two outstanding works of dystopian science fiction from the years between the world wars, themselves highly influenced by Wells, *We* (1920) by Yevgeny Zamyatin and *Brave New World* (1932) by Aldous Huxley.

We was written in Russian around 1920 but, because it was banned by the Soviet government, it did not appear until 1924 and then only in an English translation. However, it remained little known in Britain. The only copy that Orwell himself could get hold of was a French translation. In 1946 he praised the book's 'intuitive grasp of the irrational side of totalitarianism – human sacrifice, cruelty as an end in itself, the worship of a Leader who is credited with divine attributes'. Zamyatin's story is set some time after the thirtieth century in 'the One State', ruled by a terrifying figurehead called 'the Benefactor'. The people have numbers instead of names, wear identical uniforms, are under constant surveillance by the 'Guardians' and have strictly controlled sex lives. The main character keeps a diary which encourages his sense of individuality, falls in love and enters a conspiracy of rebels, but after a brainwashing operation, he betrays his lover and watches her being put to death. Although Orwell was not influenced by Zamyatin's adventurous and original style of writing, which does not seem to have survived the translation, he clearly took many components of his **plot** from the Russian masterpiece.

CHECK THE BOOK

Yevgeny Zamyatin's *We* (1920) is probably the novel which most influenced *Nineteen Eighty-Four*. There is a detailed account of how Zamyatin and Wells influenced Orwell in *The Future as Nightmare: H. G. Wells and the Anti-Utopians* by Mark Hillegas (1967).

Brave New World, published in 1932, supplied further ideas and must also have helped clarify Orwell's key themes. He took an especial interest in the views of its author, Aldous Huxley, because he had been a pupil of Huxley's when the latter taught at Eton. Huxley **satirises** trends in the modern world which are eroding the idea of human beings as unique individuals responsible for their own affairs. His twenty-fifth-century World State is a regime which deliberately uses modern science to intensify these trends. Society is divided into rigid classes, ruled by an elite of intellectuals who deprive even themselves of knowledge and freedom and who abolish genuine art, scientific research and history. Normal human feelings are replaced by artificial ones. The family is abolished in order to wipe out private emotions. Huxley speculates on the future development of television as a means of social control and on the use of cinema as a purveyor of sick fantasy, contrasted with writing as a potentially more authentic way to explore experience. (In this respect, Helmholtz's poetry has an equivalent function to Winston's diary.) Language is deliberately altered to redirect thinking, although Orwell elaborates this idea and makes it more central to his book. His Two Minutes Hate is a more aggressive version of Huxley's Solidarity Service. O'Brien, an apparently sympathetic but finally all-powerful manipulator, is a more villainous version of Huxley's Mustapha Mond, the Resident Controller for Western Europe. Less obviously, Winston's sexual frustration and fixation on a woman whose outlook is very different from his own recalls the relationship between John the Savage and Lenina. Orwell had serious reservations about Huxley's dystopia, which he felt was 'a brilliant caricature of the present' rather than a likely prediction of the future, but he valued its cynical questioning of what constituted progress and he was willing to adapt some of its features for his own book. *Brave New World* opens with a sentence which, by describing a thirty-four-storey building as 'squat', disturbs the readers and makes them feel they are reading about a very strange world. Orwell follows exactly the same path by describing the clocks striking thirteen.

These are Orwell's main sources, though there are a number of others which are significant, such as Jack London's tale of a future dictatorship, *The Iron Heel* (1908); and Arthur Koestler's novel of a

CHECK THE BOOK
Brave New World by Aldous Huxley (1932) is the only dystopia whose fame possibly equals that of *Nineteen Eighty-Four*.

prisoner under totalitarianism, *Darkness at Noon* (1940). Students who compare *Nineteen Eighty-Four* and another book should take care to do more than simply list their contents, because the success of any work of fiction depends on storytelling skill as much as on ideas. Despite all the similarities between *Nineteen Eighty-Four* and *Brave New World*, for instance, the books 'feel' very different from each other, and one reason for this is the techniques of narration. Huxley gives us a detached, satirical view of his characters by using several points of view and creating situations which prevent us identifying with anyone too closely, whereas Orwell ensures that we see the world almost entirely through Winston's eyes, experiencing the horror of life in '1984' intimately and intensively.

? QUESTION

Compare and contrast Orwell's aims and methods in creating his dystopian society with those employed by another author (e.g. Aldous Huxley or Margaret Atwood).

World events	George Orwell's life	Literary events
		1896 H. G. Wells, *The Island of Doctor Moreau*
		1899 H. G. Wells, *When the Sleeper Wakes*
1901 Death of Queen Victoria		**1902** Joseph Conrad, *Heart of Darkness*
	1903 Eric Blair born on 25 June in Bengal	
	1904 Moves to England	
		1908 Jack London, *The Iron Heel*
	1911–16 Attends St Cyprian's	
		1913 D. H. Lawrence, *Sons and Lovers*
1914 Outbreak of First World War		**1914** James Joyce, *Dubliners*
		1916 Franz Kafka, *Metamorphosis*
1917 Russian Revolution	**1917–21** Attends Eton	
1918 First World War ends; votes for women		
1919 Amritsar Massacre in Punjab		
		1920 Yevgeny Zamyatin, *We*
1922 Mussolini comes to power in Italy; inauguration of USSR	**1922** Joins Indian Imperial Police	**1922** T. S. Eliot, *The Waste Land*; James Joyce, *Ulysses*
1924 Labour Party takes office in Britain for the first time; Lenin dies		
1926 General Strike in the UK		
	1927 Resigns from police	**1927** Virginia Woolf, *To the Lighthouse*
	1928–9 Lives in Paris	**1928** D. H. Lawrence, *Lady Chatterley's Lover*
1932 British Union of Fascists launched		**1932** Aldous Huxley, *Brave New World*
1933 Over 2,500,000 unemployed men in Britain; Hitler appointed chancellor in Germany	**1933** *Down and Out in Paris and London*	
	1934 *Burmese Days*	

World events	George Orwell's life	Literary events
	1935 *A Clergyman's Daughter*	
1936–9 Spanish Civil War	**1936** *Keep the Aspidistra Flying*	
	1936–7 Orwell and his new wife, Eileen O'Shaughnessy, move to Spain and support the Republicans	
	1937 *The Road to Wigan Pier*; goes to Morocco	
	1938 *Homage to Catalonia*	
1939 Russia and Germany sign a non-aggression pact	**1939** *Coming Up for Air*; returns to England; joins the Home Guard	**1939** James Joyce, *Finnegans Wake*; John Steinbeck, *The Grapes of Wrath*
1940 Battle of Britain	**1940** *Inside the Whale*	**1940** Arthur Koestler, *Darkness at Noon*
1941 Germany invades Russia; USA joins Allies	**1941** *The Lion and the Unicorn*; becomes producer and writer for BBC	
1943 Tehran Conference	**1943** Leaves BBC and Home Guard; becomes editor of *Tribune*	
	1944 Adopts a son	
1945 Labour government in Britain	**1945** *Animal Farm*; Eileen dies suddenly	
1945–89 Cold War		
1946 Winston Churchill coins the term 'Iron Curtain'	**1946** Moves to Jura; *Critical Essays*	
	1948 *Nineteen Eighty-Four* completed; Orwell ill with tuberculosis	
	1949 *Nineteen Eighty-Four* published; marries Sonia Brownell	
	1950 Dies 21 January	
		1953 Arthur Miller, *The Crucible*
		1985 Margaret Atwood, *The Handmaid's Tale*

TEXTS OF THE NOVEL

Nineteen Eighty-Four, introduced by Ben Pimlott, Penguin, 1989
  This is the edition of the text used in preparation of these Notes

Complete Works of George Orwell, Vol. 9, edited by Peter Davison, Secker & Warburg, 1987

Nineteen Eighty-Four, edited by Bernard Crick, Clarendon Press, 1984

CRITICISM

Katherine Anne Ackley, ed., *Misogyny in Literature: An Essay Collection*, Garland, 1992

Keith Alldritt, *The Making of George Orwell*, Arnold, 1969

Harold Bloom, ed., *Modern Critical Interpretations: Nineteen Eighty-Four*, Chelsea House, 1986

Harold Bloom, ed., *Modern Critical Views: George Orwell*, Chelsea House, 1987

Peter Buitenhuis and Ira Nadel, eds., *George Orwell: A Reassessment*, Macmillan, 1988

Jenni Calder, *Chronicles of Conscience: A Study of George Orwell and Arthur Koestler*, Secker & Warburg, 1968

Jenni Calder, *Aldous Huxley and George Orwell: Brave New World and Nineteen Eighty-Four*, Arnold, 1976

Michael Carter, *George Orwell and the Problem of Authentic Existence*, Croom Helm, 1985

Roger Fowler, *The Language of George Orwell*, Macmillan, 1995

Erika Gottlieb, *The Orwell Conundrum: A Cry of Despair or Faith in the Spirit of Man?*, Carleton University Press, 1992

Mark R. Hillegas, *The Future as Nightmare: H. G. Wells and the Anti-Utopians*, Oxford University Press, 1967

Christopher Hitchens, *Orwell's Victory*, Penguin, 2002

Graham Holderness, Bryan Loughrey and Nahem Yousaf, eds., *New Casebooks: George Orwell*, Macmillan, 1998

Lynette Hunter, *George Orwell: The Search for a Voice*, Open University Press, 1984

Samuel Hynes, ed., *Twentieth-Century Interpretations of Nineteen Eighty-Four*, Prentice-Hall, 1971

Krishan Kumar, *Utopia and Anti-Utopia in Modern Times*, Blackwell Publishers, 1987

Scott Lucas, *The Betrayal of Dissent: Beyond Orwell, Hitchens and the New American Century*, Pluto Press Ltd, 2004

Jeffrey Meyers, *A Reader's Guide to George Orwell*, Thames & Hudson, 1975

Valerie Meyers, *Modern Novelists: George Orwell*, Macmillan, 1991

John Newsinger, *Orwell's Politics*, Palgrave Macmillan, 1999

Christopher Norris, ed., *Inside the Myth: Orwell – Views from the Left*, Lawrence & Wishart Ltd, 1984

Bernard Oldsey and Joseph Browne, eds., *Critical Essays on George Orwell*, Prentice-Hall, 1986

Daphne Patai, *The Orwell Mystique: Study in Male Ideology*, University of Massachusetts Press, 1984

Alok Rai, *Orwell and the Politics of Despair: A Critical Study of the Writings of George Orwell*, Cambridge University Press, 1988

Richard Rees, *George Orwell: Fugitive from the Camp of Victory*, Secker & Warburg, 1961

Patrick Reilly, *George Orwell: The Age's Adversary*, Macmillan, 1986

Patrick Reilly, *The Literature of Guilt: From Gulliver to Golding*, Macmillan, 1988

Patrick Reilly, *Nineteen Eighty-Four: Past, Present and Future*, Twayne, 1989

Jonathan Rose, ed., *The Revised Orwell*, Michigan State University Press, 1992

Alan Sandison, *The Last Man in Europe: Essay on George Orwell*, Macmillan, 1974 (later revised as *George Orwell: After 1984*, Macmillan, 1986)

Christopher Small, *The Road to Miniluv: George Orwell, the State and God*, Gollancz, 1975

Richard Smyer, *Primal Dream and Primal Crime: Orwell's Development as a Psychological Novelist*, University of Missouri Press, 1979

Anthony West, *Principles and Persuasions: The Literary Essays of Anthony West*, Eyre & Spottiswoode, 1958

W. J. West, *The Larger Evils: Orwell and the Roots of Nineteen Eighty-Four*, Canongate Books Ltd, 1992

Raymond Williams, *Modern Masters: Orwell*, Collins Fontana, 1971

Raymond Williams, ed., *George Orwell: A Collection of Critical Essays*, Prentice-Hall, 1974

George Woodcock, *The Crystal Spirit: A Study of George Orwell*, Cape, 1967

David Wykes, *A Preface to Orwell*, Longman, 1987

Alex Zwerdling, *Orwell and the Left*, Yale University Press, 1974

BIOGRAPHY AND GENERAL READING

Gordon Bowker, *Inside George Orwell: A Biography*, Palgrave Macmillan, 2003

Malcolm Bradbury, *The Modern English Novel*, Secker & Warburg, 1993

Bernard Crick, *George Orwell: A Life*, Secker & Warburg, 1980

Peter Davison, *George Orwell: A Literary Life*, Macmillan, 1996

John Gribbin, *Science: A History*, Penguin, 2002

Eric Hobsbawm, *Age of Extremes: The Short Twentieth Century, 1914–1991*, Michael Joseph, 1994

Michael McKeon, ed., *Theory of the Novel: A Historical Approach*, Johns Hopkins Press, 2000

Mark Mazower, *Dark Continent: Europe's Twentieth Century*, Penguin, 1998

Martin Montgomery, Alan Durant, Nigel Fabb, Tom Furniss and Sarah Mills, *Ways of Reading: Advanced Reading Skills for Students of English Literature*, Routledge, 1992

Michael Shelden, *Orwell: The Authorised Biography*, William Heinemann, 1991

Peter Singer, *Marx: A Very Short Introduction*, Oxford University Press, 1980

D. J. Taylor, *Orwell: The Life*, Chatto & Windus, 2003

caricature (Italian 'to exaggerate') a ludicrous rendering of character, achieved by the exaggeration of appearance or behaviour

characterisation the way in which a writer creates characters so as to convey their personalities effectively, attract or repel our sympathies and integrate their behaviour into the story

comedy, comic a broad genre; the word is most often used to describe a story which is intended primarily to entertain its audience and which ends happily for the main characters. However, **satirical** comedy may be painfully unflinching in its depiction of human folly, vice and greed; and it is possible for a story to contain comic incident and effects without itself being a comedy

comic relief the inclusion of a comic scene in a story for the purpose of dramatic contrast with more serious episodes

dissolve a moment of narrative transition in cinema or television, when one scene fades away and another replaces it

distance, distancing a work of literature should arouse its reader's sympathies, but if a reader identifies too strongly with a character, situation or idea, whether for emotional, personal or political reasons, it may distort judgement. A writer may therefore create 'distance' between the reader and the events of the text, for example by commenting on the action or by giving an otherwise heroic character unsympathetic faults

dystopia an imaginary world which is worse than our own, the opposite of a utopia

fable a short tale conveying a clear moral lesson in which the characters are animals acting like human beings

foil a character who illuminates by contrast some aspects of a more central character

free indirect discourse a technique of narrating the thoughts or speech of a character by incorporating their words or ideas into a third-person narrative: 'And yet he was in the right! They were wrong and he was right' (Part One, Chapter 7, p. 84)

image, imagery in its narrowest sense, an image is a word-picture, describing some visible scene or object, such as 'the pale, cloudless sky, stretching away behind the chimney pots into interminable distances' (Part Two, Chapter 10, p. 229). More commonly, imagery refers to the figurative language (**similes** and **metaphors**) in a work of literature *in media res* the technique of starting a story 'in the middle', with events already going on, letting necessary information emerge as the story progresses

irony, ironic saying one thing while meaning another, with the true meaning to some extent contradicting the surface one. Sarcasm is a comparatively straightforward type, when someone makes a mocking statement which in the given context clearly means the reverse of what it says. More sophisticated irony can be much harder to recognise and interpret, however, because it relies on the writer and reader sharing values and knowledge. A highly ironic piece of writing may even suggest several different ways of responding to statements, characters and events, and conceal entirely the attitudes of its author

jargon technical terms which can be useful for quick, accurate communication between experts, but tend to annoy the general public

metaphor a metaphor goes further than a comparison between two different things or ideas by fusing them together: one thing is described as being another thing, carrying over its associations: 'a small knot of people' (Part Three, Chapter 6, p. 306)

motif an aspect of the text which recurs frequently, such as a word, phrase, **image**, incident or character

naturalism a type of **realism** which emphasises the influence of the environment and heredity on characters, and which tends to dwell on the sordid and miserable aspects of life, depicting people as animals driven by their appetites and by forces beyond their control

parody an imitation of something, for example a style of writing or a particular work of literature, intended to ridicule its characteristic features

pastoral an imaginary world of simple, idealised rural life

plot the plan of a literary work. More than the simple sequence of events, 'plot' suggests a pattern of relationships between events: a story with a beginning, middle and end, with its various parts bound together by cause and effect, exhibiting a version of typical experience or a view of morality. Suspense is vital to make a plot entertaining: we should be made to want to know what is going to happen, and be surprised by new incidents, yet be satisfied that they grow logically out of what we already know

realism a vague term, but one it is difficult to do without. Often associated with the mainstream of fiction from the eighteenth to the twentieth centuries, realism is an approach to the writing of literature which focuses on 'everyday life'. Characters are middle or lower class; subject matter is related to normal experience; description picks out details in a 'documentary' way; plot dashes characters' 'unrealistic' hopes. No book can be entirely realistic, if only because it is made out of words, but it can be more or less realistic

register language which is appropriate to a particular situation, such as the language of courtship or the language of law

rhetoric the art of speaking or writing effectively so as to persuade an audience, and the devices of language used to achieve this

rhetorical question a statement which is put in the form of a question in order to emphasise it. It does not require a reply

satire literature which exhibits and examines vice and folly and makes them appear ridiculous or contemptible. Satire differs from straightforward comedy in having a purpose, using laughter to attack its objects

science fiction literature about imaginary marvels or disasters created by future scientific discoveries and technological developments

simile an explicit comparison in which one thing is said to be like another. Similes always contain the words 'like' or 'as': 'Hatred would fill him like an enormous roaring flame' (Part Three, Chapter 4, p. 294)

stereotype, stereotypical something which conforms to a standard, fixed idea. The word can be used pejoratively, to indicate an ordinary, commonplace perception which has been made dull by frequent repetition, a person or event so ordinary that it conforms to such an expectation, or a prejudiced view of someone which falsely assumes that they fit the expectation. The word may also be used neutrally, to signify stock characters, ideas and situations which are the typical material of literature

surrealism a movement in the visual arts and literature between the two world wars, which tried to bypass reason and produce words and images as directly as possible from the 'subconscious'. Surrealist writing has the coherence of a dream, rather than of a story or other normal structure

symbol, symbolic something which represents something else (often an idea or quality) either by analogy or association.

tragedy, tragic a story which traces the downfall of an individual, and in so doing shows both the capacities and the limitations of human life

Michael Sherborne is Curriculum Manager of English and Humanities at Luton Sixth Form College. He is the author of the York Notes Advanced on *A Midsummer Night's Dream* (2000) and *Brave New World* (2000). He has edited *The Country of the Blind and Other Stories by H. G. Wells* (Oxford University Press, 1996, not available in the EC) and is also the author – under the name Michael Draper – of *Modern Novelists: H. G. Wells* (Macmillan, 1987).

General editor

Martin Gray, former Head of the Department of English Studies at the University of Stirling, and of Literary Studies at the University of Luton

Maya Angelou
I Know Why the Caged Bird Sings

Jane Austen
Pride and Prejudice

Alan Ayckbourn
Absent Friends

Elizabeth Barrett Browning
Selected Poems

Robert Bolt
A Man for All Seasons

Harold Brighouse
Hobson's Choice

Charlotte Brontë
Jane Eyre

Emily Brontë
Wuthering Heights

Shelagh Delaney
A Taste of Honey

Charles Dickens
David Copperfield
Great Expectations
Hard Times
Oliver Twist

Roddy Doyle
Paddy Clarke Ha Ha Ha

George Eliot
Silas Marner
The Mill on the Floss

Anne Frank
The Diary of a Young Girl

William Golding
Lord of the Flies

Oliver Goldsmith
She Stoops to Conquer

Willis Hall
The Long and the Short and the Tall

Thomas Hardy
Far from the Madding Crowd
The Mayor of Casterbridge
Tess of the d'Urbervilles
The Withered Arm and other Wessex Tales

L.P. Hartley
The Go-Between

Seamus Heaney
Selected Poems

Susan Hill
I'm the King of the Castle

Barry Hines
A Kestrel for a Knave

Louise Lawrence
Children of the Dust

Harper Lee
To Kill a Mockingbird

Laurie Lee
Cider with Rosie

Arthur Miller
The Crucible
A View from the Bridge

Robert O'Brien
Z for Zachariah

Frank O'Connor
My Oedipus Complex and Other Stories

George Orwell
Animal Farm

J.B. Priestley
An Inspector Calls
When We Are Married

Willy Russell
Educating Rita
Our Day Out

J.D. Salinger
The Catcher in the Rye

William Shakespeare
Henry IV Part I
Henry V
Julius Caesar
Macbeth
The Merchant of Venice
A Midsummer Night's Dream
Much Ado About Nothing

Romeo and Juliet
The Tempest
Twelfth Night

George Bernard Shaw
Pygmalion

Mary Shelley
Frankenstein

R.C. Sherriff
Journey's End

Rukshana Smith
Salt on the snow

John Steinbeck
Of Mice and Men

Robert Louis Stevenson
Dr Jekyll and Mr Hyde

Jonathan Swift
Gulliver's Travels

Robert Swindells
Daz 4 Zoe

Mildred D. Taylor
Roll of Thunder, Hear My Cry

Mark Twain
Huckleberry Finn

James Watson
Talking in Whispers

Edith Wharton
Ethan Frome

William Wordsworth
Selected Poems

A Choice of Poets

Mystery Stories of the Nineteenth Century including The Signalman

Nineteenth Century Short Stories

Poetry of the First World War

Six Women Poets

For the AQA Anthology:

Duffy and Armitage & Pre-1914 Poetry

Heaney and Clarke & Pre-1914 Poetry

Poems from Different Cultures

Margaret Atwood
Cat's Eye
The Handmaid's Tale

Jane Austen
Emma
Mansfield Park
Persuasion
Pride and Prejudice
Sense and Sensibility

Alan Bennett
Talking Heads

William Blake
Songs of Innocence and of Experience

Charlotte Brontë
Jane Eyre
Villette

Emily Brontë
Wuthering Heights

Angela Carter
Nights at the Circus

Geoffrey Chaucer
The Franklin's Prologue and Tale
The Merchant's Prologue and Tale
The Miller's Prologue and Tale
The Prologue to the Canterbury Tales
The Wife of Bath's Prologue and Tale

Samuel Coleridge
Selected Poems

Joseph Conrad
Heart of Darkness

Daniel Defoe
Moll Flanders

Charles Dickens
Bleak House
Great Expectations
Hard Times

Emily Dickinson
Selected Poems

John Donne
Selected Poems

Carol Ann Duffy
Selected Poems

George Eliot
Middlemarch
The Mill on the Floss

T.S. Eliot
Selected Poems
The Waste Land

F. Scott Fitzgerald
The Great Gatsby

E.M. Forster
A Passage to India

Brian Friel
Translations

Thomas Hardy
Jude the Obscure
The Mayor of Casterbridge
The Return of the Native
Selected Poems
Tess of the d'Urbervilles

Seamus Heaney
Selected Poems from 'Opened Ground'

Nathaniel Hawthorne
The Scarlet Letter

Homer
The Iliad
The Odyssey

Aldous Huxley
Brave New World

Kazuo Ishiguro
The Remains of the Day

Ben Jonson
The Alchemist

James Joyce
Dubliners

John Keats
Selected Poems

Philip Larkin
The Whitsun Weddings and Selected Poems

Christopher Marlowe
Doctor Faustus
Edward II

Arthur Miller
Death of a Salesman

John Milton
Paradise Lost Books I & II

Toni Morrison
Beloved

George Orwell
Nineteen Eighty-Four

Sylvia Plath
Selected Poems

Alexander Pope
Rape of the Lock & Selected Poems

William Shakespeare
Antony and Cleopatra
As You Like It
Hamlet
Henry IV Part I
King Lear
Macbeth
Measure for Measure
The Merchant of Venice
A Midsummer Night's Dream
Much Ado About Nothing
Othello
Richard II
Richard III
Romeo and Juliet
The Taming of the Shrew
The Tempest
Twelfth Night
The Winter's Tale

George Bernard Shaw
Saint Joan

Mary Shelley
Frankenstein

Jonathan Swift
Gulliver's Travels and A Modest Proposal

Alfred Tennyson
Selected Poems

Virgil
The Aeneid

Alice Walker
The Color Purple

Oscar Wilde
The Importance of Being Earnest

Tennessee Williams
A Streetcar Named Desire
The Glass Menagerie

Jeanette Winterson
Oranges Are Not the Only Fruit

John Webster
The Duchess of Malfi

Virginia Woolf
To the Lighthouse

William Wordsworth
The Prelude and Selected Poems

W.B. Yeats
Selected Poems

Metaphysical Poets